Advaita Made Easy

The answer to the question
'Who am I?'

Advaita
Made Easy

The answer to the question
'Who am I?'

Dennis Waite

BOOKS

Winchester, UK
Washington, USA

First published by O-Books, 2012
O-Books is an imprint of John Hunt Publishing Ltd., Laurel House, Station Approach,
Alresford, Hants, SO24 9JH, UK
office1@jhpbooks.net
www.johnhuntpublishing.com

For distributor details and how to order please visit the 'Ordering' section on our website.

ISBN: 978 1 78099 184 9

A CIP catalogue record for this book is available from the British Library.

Design: Stuart Davies

Printed and bound by CPI Group (UK) Ltd, Croydon, CR0 4YY

We operate a distinctive and ethical publishing philosophy in all
areas of our business, from our global network of authors to
production and worldwide distribution.

CONTENTS

What is Advaita?

Introduction

Whenever anyone asks me what I do, they are initially interested when I say that I am a writer but, as soon as they ask what sort of books I write and I answer they are about an Indian philosophy called Advaita, they usually do not ask any more questions. If they do, attempting to provide a response in just a few sentences is likely to give the impression that I am an eccentric who never grew out of the hippie culture.

This is a great pity and the impression is quite erroneous (I was never a hippy). The teaching of Advaita is several thousand years old and is a proven methodology for discovering the nature of your Self and that of the world. And the realization of the fundamental truth that is presented reduces all other considerations to complete insignificance.

I have now written several books on the subject but most of my family and friends cannot be bothered to read them. So there is clearly a need for a short book that gives the essential answer to that question 'What is Advaita?' without requiring too much effort on the part of the reader. This is that book.

Meaning

The word Advaita is a Sanskrit term (note that there is a Glossary at the end of the book containing brief definition of all Sanskrit terms); 'dvaita' means 'duality' and the prefix 'a' in front of a Sanskrit word negates it, so 'advaita' means 'not duality'. So this book could be really short. It could consist of a single sentence: "In reality, there are not two things." The problem is that such a sentence would not satisfactorily answer the question. This is because such a statement is clearly contrary to all of our experience – we know that there are lots of things! And, although you may not yet realize this, all of our dissatisfaction and unhappiness results from our mistaken belief in duality. We know that we are not happy for a large part of the time; we know that we are going to die. And so on.

And, if I simply tell you that you are mistaken, that you do not really 'know' these things; that all of your experience only relates to how things appear to be, you are most unlikely even to consider the possibility. So all of this needs to be explained, simply but gradually, one step at a time. If you agree with the logical reasoning of each step, then you will be obliged to consider the conclusion seriously, too.

Origin

Advaita is best thought of as a teaching method rather than a philosophy, although pedantically it is one of the schools of one of the six branches of Hindu philosophy. This particular branch, called Uttara Mimamsa, derives its teaching from the latter part of the massive body of scriptures called the Vedas. These contain the Upanishads, which form the principal source material for Advaita. There are two other major sources, both of which are actually based upon the Upanishads as well. One is called the Bhagavad Gita, itself part of the much larger, famous, epic poem called the Mahabharata. The other is a philosophical text , called the Brahma Sutra, which is intended to answer doubts and objections about what is said in the other two. To be strictly accurate, the Vedas themselves constitute a 'source of knowledge' which cannot be obtained from anywhere else. In order to be able truly to understand what they are telling us, however, we need a teacher who has learned the method of interpreting them from his teacher.

The classical belief is that the knowledge conveyed by the

2

Vedas arose at the same time as the creation itself and it was certainly the case that the words themselves were passed down orally from teacher to disciple long before the written word gained prominence. There still exists a complex formal procedure for learning the words by heart in such a way as to avoid error. Accordingly, the knowledge is said to be 'revealed' knowledge, not of human origin. In the West, we seem to have the idea that we have continually to develop and refine past knowledge or at least adapt it to our particular time or society. In the case of those who teach and study Advaita, the purpose is to preserve it intact. Why? Because it enables us to realize the nature of ourselves and reality; to recognize that we are perfect and complete.

And this is crucial to the understanding of the teaching. The scriptures are not a source of information or knowledge in the sense that a textbook on Chemistry might be considered to be. Correctly handled by a teacher, the words function to give us direct recognition of the nature of ourselves and reality. This is not mere, intellectual knowledge; it destroys self-ignorance.

The Advaitic interpretation of the scriptures was systematized by arguably one of the greatest ever philosophers - Shankara, in around the 8th - 9th century AD. He wrote commentaries on the major Upanishads, the Bhagavad Gita and Brahma Sutra and also wrote a number of self-contained texts to explain aspects of the teaching. He travelled India, defeating in rational argument all comers from other philosophies and set up centers of teaching which have survived until today. And, despite achieving all of this, he died at the age of only 32.

Strictly speaking, only the teaching as clarified by Shankara should be called 'Advaita Vedanta'. Other philosophers have made modifications to varying degrees over the centuries since his death and this means that there are divergent interpretations. This book will aim to present the understanding according to Shankara.

What does it say?

We presently experience ourselves as separate persons in a universe of objects. Despite the seeming duality that we experience, according to Advaita reality is actually non-dual. This non-dual reality is called Brahman. As a matter of fact we do feel ourselves to be other than our body or mind. Advaita calls our essential self, which is beyond body and mind, the Atman. And it teaches that this Atman is Brahman, which is non-dual.

There is an oft-quoted sentence which is said to summarize Shankara's teaching. This is:

> *brahma satyam, jaganmithyA, jIvo brahmaiva nAparah* (Shankara spoke Sanskrit and this is the Romanized equivalent of that sentence.) Translated, it means: "Brahman is the reality; the world is not in itself real; the individual self is not different from Brahman."

This will all be explained later, you will be pleased to hear!

There are other non-dual philosophies, such as Zen, Taoism, Dzogchen. Even Christianity, Islam and Judaism all have their non-dual branches. But traditional Advaita is unique in having a 'two-level' approach to reality. Whereas many teachings attempt to impose a non-dual understanding from the beginning, when this is clearly counter-intuitive, Advaita accepts that we perceive and understand our experience as dualistic and begins the teaching from there.

(The differences between the traditional teaching of Advaita and other more recent variants will hopefully become clearer by the end of the book. Briefly, traditional teaching requires mental preparedness and utilizes the Vedantic scriptures as source material, though this needs to be 'unfolded' by a qualified teacher in a methodical and structured manner. Modern, Western 'satsang' teaching claims that none of these are necessary, which is why it does not work very well, if at all!)

Terminology

To be strictly accurate (and it is one of the purposes of this book to give you the correct picture, rather than the many books around that are likely to mislead you), I should really refer to 'Advaita Vedanta', rather than simply 'Advaita'. 'Vedanta' is a noun referring to the words or teachings that occur at the end (Sanskrit 'anta') of the Vedas, i.e. the Upanishads. Advaita is an adjective describing the nature of that teaching. There are other philosophies that extract a dualistic or mixed message from these scriptural texts but 'Advaita Vedanta' indicates that the content of the message is that the nature of reality is 'Advaita' – non-dual. There are also many teachers today who use the word Advaita when what they are teaching clearly does not derive from the words of the Upanishads, which in the hands of a qualified teacher, are guaranteed to lead a mentally prepared student to enlightenment.

Throughout this book, I will be using the word 'Advaita' somewhat loosely, because this is how it has come to be used in the West. I will, for example, use phrases such as 'Advaita teaches' or 'According to Advaita'. In both these case, I ought strictly to use 'Advaita Vedanta', meaning that variant of Vedanta which understands reality to be non-dual.

2

How ought we to act?

Desire, Action and Results

Life is a never-ending cycle of desires followed by actions followed by results (usually disappointing ones because we expected too much). It is a cycle because, once we have attained the desired objective, we quickly supplant the old desire by a new one and the process begins again. We thought that we would be happy when we got whatever it was that we believed that we wanted – and indeed this is often the case. But unfortunately, it does not last – it always turns out that we were mistaken about its ultimate value.

Why do we do it? It is because we feel that we are limited in some way and that the desired object will make us complete. This applies to all desires, from the most basic to the most sophisticated. But there is only one desire which, once satisfied, will bring us the fulfillment that we seek and that is to realize our true nature. This is because that realization will bring with it the discovery that we are in fact unlimited. We are already complete.

The Bhagavad Gita tells us that thinking about objects leads to attachment and we then want to have them. If we are thwarted in this, we become angry. This progresses to delusion, confusion and loss of reason – we are then lost.

Advaita recognizes the existence of a kind of moral law that operates in the universe, it is called 'dharma' (but this is a big subject and not one which I will address in this book). The effect of this is that, when our actions are in accord with dharma, we gain 'merit points'; when they go against dharma, we gain 'demerit'. So, as a general rule, we could say that actions which help society, other people, the environment etc result in merit, while actions which injure others or ourselves bring demerit. If the motive fits in with this attitude, we can avoid satisfaction or guilt and simply accept whatever happens.

All our actions will inevitably have their consequence at some time in the future, since there is a cause-effect relationship, just as with physical laws of action and reaction. This can be easily understood at the gross level. Living a profligate and indulgent lifestyle, for example, may give pleasure now but will probably lead to regret as the body rebels in later life. But it applies to the subtle world of thought and motive, also.

Karma and Reincarnation

This, then, is the theory of 'karma'. Karma is effectively another word for the law of cause and effect. We know that, if we apply heat to a kettle full of cold water, it will eventually boil and turn into steam. If we kick something, it may fly into the air or bruise our toe, depending upon its inertia - but there will be an effect. The law of karma says that everything we do will have an effect; maybe not straight away but eventually, even if in a subsequent life. And the law applies to all of our actions, not just the simply physical.

We often note how some people seem to have no concern for others, spending vast sums of money on themselves without (in our view) really having done anything to earn it. And, at the same time, we see some who devote their lives to the service of others and yet live in relative poverty themselves. And we ask 'where is the justice in this?'

Now, before you read the next section, please bear in mind that what I am about to say is not the final teaching of Advaita. So, if you cannot countenance the idea of gods or reincarnation, do not worry too much. Just read on! It will take a while for the total picture to become clear.

The basic teaching of advaita tells us that, over the course of our lives, these good and bad points accumulate – these 'points' are called karmas or sanskaras, and, although they may not come to fruition in *this* life (so that the bad people get their comeuppance), they will eventually do so, since reincarnation forms a part of the teaching. This means that we are born into a situation appropriate to a subset of our accumulated karma. If we have been very bad in a previous life (not necessarily the one immediately preceding), this may entail being born as a lower life form, such as a cockroach. The word for the package of situations we encounter in this life – be they the cause of happiness or the opposite – is prarabdha. The human form is not quite the highest, since there are also celestial beings in heavenly realms. But is by far the most important, since it is the only form in which one can escape this cycle of birth and death, which is called 'samsara'.

Goals of Life

Escape from samsara, the 'eternal round of birth and death', is achieved by becoming 'enlightened'. More will be said about this later but, briefly, it means recognizing the true nature of oneself and reality (i.e. being non-dual). Once this has been achieved, one lives out the remainder of one's life (thereby exhausting the sanskara that brought it about) but is then born no more. This may seem like it is not especially desirable but there is rather more to it than that, as you will shortly see.

Thus it is, that the goals in human life are divided into four by traditional advaita:

1. The first of these relates to the basic necessities of life and the means for obtaining these. Until we have these, we are never going to think about looking for enlightenment!

2. The second goal relates to satisfaction of personal desires, whether crude or refined - obtaining those things that give me pleasure.

3. Once I have satisfied my own needs, only then can I start to think about others. Living within society, I have responsibilities within the community and outside. We could think of this as a series of concentric circles, with myself at the centre and the human race at the edge, and with a decreasing importance as we move outwards.

   As noted above, we gain brownie points as a result of doing good deeds so that, in one sense, such activities also benefit myself eventually in that an accumulation of good sanskara will improve my prospects for the next life.

4. A few people eventually realize that the pursuance of the above three goals is ultimately unfulfilling. The house falls into disrepair; clothes become frayed and holey; the satisfaction following a good meal soon grows into renewed hunger. The fulfillment of those basic needs is an eternally ongoing process. Similarly, the enjoyment following a satisfied desire is invariably short lived. And, no matter how many people we help, there are innumerable others still in need. What we want ultimately is the freedom from needs of any kind, all of the time. This is the ultimate goal - it is called 'moksha'.

Free Will

Whenever we talk about action, it is inevitable that we must eventually address the topic of free-will. We all know that it feels as though we have (at least some) freedom of choice but what does Advaita have to say on the matter?

Although, the subject itself is quite complex, the fundamentals can be summarized quite easily. When we 'choose', the so-called choice may be the result of:

1. **Fate or Destiny**. This means that the choice itself, as well as the result, is bound to happen no matter what we do.

The entire unfolding of creation has been 'set out' in concrete since it began.

2. **Determinism.** This means that the choice and the result can be traced to prior causes. There is no freedom in our choice, which is invariably determined by genetic and environmental aspects.

3. **Free will.** Although we are clearly influenced by past events, by our particular personalities and by the present circumstances, we are able to choose to act or not, and how to act, within the limitations of our personal capacity.

According to Advaita, our scope for action is limited by our past karma but, within those restrictions, we do have free will. So this coincides with what we might regard as the 'common sense' view. We are also constrained by the laws of creation. E.g. we might choose to fly to work under our own power but the law of gravity and construction of the human body prevent us. One metaphor used is that of a motor boat in a fast flowing river. The current of the river will tend to take the boat with it but there is limited scope for maneuver and directing our journey; and the more powerful the motor (i.e. determination), the better we can counter the flow.

As will be seen later, at the empirical level (i.e. the world as it seems to us in our day-to-day life), Advaita accepts the existence of individual persons and a 'creator' and 'ruler' of the universe called Ishvara. Ishvara is the name given to the totality of the laws that govern how the creation 'works' and, in particular in this context, He is responsible for giving us our bodies in this life, according to the accumulated sanskara from previous lives. Thus, we can say that action is, in a sense, a 'joint' effort. Ishvara manifests the world to meet the needs of the global karma from previous creations, which itself was generated as a result of our past actions. And we act within the context and limitations imposed by the natural laws of the creation brought about by Ishvara. Thus, at this level, both we and Ishvara can be said to 'act' (and 'enjoy' the result of our actions). (In reality, neither acts because neither exists as a separate entity - but the explanations for that statement will come later!)

Our actions are therefore mostly triggered by pre-determined prarabdha but we have some free-will. Since we cannot know which will be effective in any instance, we have to assume free-will and endeavor to ensure that we act in accord with dharma.

3

What is real and what is illusion?

Probably the major problem confronting the person who is first told about Advaita is the claim that reality is 'non-dual'. This is often stated as 'There are not two things', which may seem to be less than no help at all! To claim that the universe, including all animate and animate things in it, are all essentially the same is so blatantly in contravention of our everyday experience that the hearer is inclined to reject the notion out of hand.

I am presently sitting in front of a keyboard and computer screen, typing these words. Clearly 'I' am not either of these things. 'I' am separate from them. I can walk away slowly from them and see them getting further away. As I leave the room, I can look before I close the door and they are still there. I can then leave the house altogether; the monitor and keyboard are nowhere to be seen. Yet, when I return, there they are; just as I left them (hopefully)! How can it be in any way meaningful to say that my 'essential Self' and the 'essential' nature of the keyboard are 'one and the same'?

Waking versus Dream

One way of beginning to think about this, and to see that maybe it is not so ludicrous, is to consider your dreams. You have dreams in which you live an entirely different life, interacting with people who probably do not exist, visiting places that you have never been to in your waking life and doing things that you would probably never normally consider doing. Yet you do not question this at the time of the dream - you take it for reality. It is only after waking up that you realize it was all a product of your own imagination.

But dreams are not comparable with the waking reality, you might say. And you might put forward some arguments as to why this is - and these might seem perfectly reasonable at first sight. Some such arguments are as follows.

1. Dreams are not realistic, once you look at them more closely. Things happen illogically and in contravention of the laws of physics. For example one can travel to another country in seconds. (But, when you wake up, you find that you are still lying on your bed.) All of the fantastic things that one sees, including many that could not even exist in reality, are inside one's head (and one's head is not big enough to contain them).

But these observations are from the waker's standpoint, after awakening from the dream. It has to be appreciated that it is not the waker who has the dream experience. The 'waker ego' and the 'dreamer ego' have to be regarded as separate entities. For the dreamer, *only* the dream objects are real; the so-called 'real, waking world objects' do not even exist. Time 'really' passes in the dream and movement takes place in 'real' space.

You may have to think about the above argument for some considerable time. We are so used to considering that the waking world is 'real' and the dream world 'unreal', that we may not initially accept the idea of a 'dreamer ego'. You have to keep bringing yourself back to the appreciation that it is the 'waking ego' that is doing all of the assessment and making this judgment. But you also know that this 'waking ego' is not there in the dream!

2. We often attempt to rationalize the unreality of dreams in this way, by claiming that 'it is all inside our head'. Things in the 'real' (i.e. waking) world exist independently of us and other people can see them. Obviously (and perhaps

fortunately) other people do not see what happens in my dreams.

But this is again looking at the situation from the vantage point of the waker. From his viewpoint, the dream world is indeed 'inside' his head. But, from the vantage point of the dreamer, the dream world is very much 'outside'. Indeed, the dreamer is not dreaming at all, from his point of view; he is very much awake. In theory, the dreamer could go to sleep, within the dream, and have a second-order dream. When he subsequently wakes up, into the first dream, it is precisely analogous to the ordinary dreamer waking up. How do we know that, when we 'really' awake in the morning, it is not into a third-order dream? What we perceive as being 'outside' is not necessarily real at all.

Another way of looking at this would be to claim that our dream world is only 'subjective', while the waking world is 'objective'. Other people can see my computer and keyboard after I have left the room. But this does not help, since the 'other people' *in my dream* can also still see my dream computer when I am not there. The dream computer and people are only realized to have been part of a 'subjective' world after I wake up.

3. You can actually 'do' things when you are awake and what you do has an actual 'effect'. What you appear to do in dreams has no effect whatsoever.

But this is again confusing the 'waker' ego with the 'dreamer'. The dreamer might be desperately thirsty, for example. The real body of the waker, might be lying on a bed next to a pitcher of cold water and a glass but these are of no use at all to the dreamer; all that can satisfy him is a 'dream drink'. The sleeper might have eaten a large meal before retiring yet be starving hungry in the dream. And he will have to eat a second (dream) meal to satisfy that hunger.

All of this tells us that what seems to be very real may turn out to be unreal if and when viewed from another vantage point. The world is not *absolutely* real; it is only *relatively* real.

Mithya

This leads us on to one of the most important concepts in Advaita, and it is best introduced by a story that I originally wrote to explain what is meant by the word 'Advaita':

"So, Swami-ji, what would you say that Advaita is?" The eager young woman crossed her legs and sat expectantly, pencil poised above a pristine pad of paper.

"It simply means 'not two' – the ultimate truth is non-dual," replied the Sage, reclining in a large and comfortable-looking armchair and not sitting in an upright lotus position, as he ought to have been, for the sake of the photograph that she had just taken, if nothing else.

She continued to wait for further elucidation before beginning to write but it soon became apparent that the answer had been given. "But is it a religion? Do you believe in God, for example?"

"Ah, well, that would depend upon what you mean by those words, wouldn't it?" he responded, irritatingly. "If, by 'religion', you mean does it have priests and churches and a band of followers who are prepared to kill non-believers, then the answer is no. If, on the other hand, you refer to the original, literal meaning of the word, namely to 'bind again', to reunite the mistaken person that we think we are with the Self that we truly are, then yes, it is a religion. Similarly, if by 'God' you mean a separate, supernatural being who created the universe and will reward us by sending us to heaven if we do what He wants, then the answer is no. If you use the term in the sense of the unmanifest, non-dual reality, then yes, I most certainly do believe in God."

The pencil raced across the paper, recording the answer for the benefit of the magazine's readers but, as the words clashed with previous ideas in her memory, the lack of a clear resolution of her questions was reflected by an increasing puzzlement in her expression.

He registered this with compassion and held out his hand towards her. "Give me a piece of paper from your pad."

She looked up, mouth slightly open as she wondered why he could possibly want that. But she turned the pad over, carefully tore off the bottom sheet and placed it in his outstretched hand. He turned to the table at his right and deftly began to fold and refold the paper. After a few moments, he turned back and, before she had had time to see what he had done, he held the paper aloft and launched it into the air. It rose quickly and circled gracefully around the room before losing momentum and diving to meet a sudden end when its pointed nose hit a sauce bottle on the dining table. "Could you bring it back over here do you think?" he asked.

"So, what would you say that we have here?" he asked, as she handed it back to him.

"It's a paper airplane," she replied, with just a hint of questioning in her voice, since the answer was so obvious that she felt he must have some other purpose in mind.

"Really?" he responded and, in an instant, he screwed up the object and, with a practiced, over-arm movement, threw it effortlessly in a wide arc, from which it landed just short of the waste paper basket in the corner of the room. "And now?" he asked.

"It's a screwed-up ball of paper", she said, without any doubt in her voice this time.

"Could you bring it back again, please", he continued. She did so, wondering if this was typical of such an interview, spending the session chasing about after bits of paper like a dog running after a stick. He took the ball and carefully unfolded it, spread it out on the table and smoothed his hand over it a few times before handing it back to her. "And now it is just a sheet of paper again," he said, "although I'm afraid it's a bit crumpled now!"

He looked at her, apparently anticipating some sign of understanding if not actual revelation but none was forthcoming. He looked around the room and, after a moment, he stood up, walked over to the window and removed a rose from a vase standing in the alcove. Returning to his seat, he held the rose out to her and asked, "What is this?"

She was feeling increasingly embarrassed as it was clear he was trying to explain something fundamental, which she was not understanding. Either that or he was mad or deliberately provoking her, neither of which seemed likely, since he remained calm and open and somehow intensely present. "It's a flower," she replied eventually.

He then deliberately took one of the petals between his right-hand thumb and fore-finger and plucked it. He looked at her and said, "And now?" She didn't reply, though it seemed that this time he didn't really expect an answer. He continued to remove the petals one by one until none remained, looking up at her after each action. Finally, he pulled the remaining parts of the flower head off the stem and dropped them onto the floor, leaving the bare stalk, which he held out to her. "Where is the flower now?" he asked. Receiving no reply, he bent down and picked up all of the petals, eventually displaying them in his open hand. "Is this a flower?" he asked.

She shook her head slowly. "It was a flower only when all of the petals and the other bits were all attached to the stem."

"Good!" he said, appreciatively. "Flower is the name that we give to that particular arrangement of all of the parts. Once we have separated it into its component parts, the flower ceases to exist. But was there ever an actual, separate thing called 'flower'? All of the material that constituted the original form is still here in these parts in my hand.

"The paper airplane is an even simpler example. There never was an airplane was there? And I don't just mean that it was only a toy. There was only ever paper. To begin with, the paper was in the form of a flat sheet for writing on. Then, I folded it in various ways so that it took on an aerodynamic shape which could fly through the air slowly. The name that we give to that form is 'airplane'. When I screwed it up, the ball-shape could be thrown more accurately. 'Airplane' and 'ball' were names relating to particular forms of the paper but at all times, all that ever actually existed was paper.

"Now, this sort of analysis applies to every 'thing' that you care to think of. Look at that table over there and this chair on which you are sitting. What are they made of? You will probably say that they are wooden chairs?"

He looked at her questioningly and she nodded, knowing at the same time that he was going to contradict her.

"Well, they are made of wood certainly, but that does not mean that they are wooden chairs! On the contrary, I would say that this, that you are sitting on, is actually chairy wood, and that object over there is tably wood. What do you say to that?"

"You mean that the thing that we call 'chair' is just a name that we give to the wood when it is that particular shape and being used for that particular function?" she asked, with understanding beginning to dawn.

"Exactly! I couldn't have put it better myself. It is quite possible that I could have a bag full of pieces of wood that can be slotted together in different ways so that at one time I might assemble them into something to sit upon, another time into something to put food upon and so on. We give the various forms distinct names and we forget that they are ONLY names and forms and not distinct and separate things.

"Look – here's an apple," he said, picking one out of the bowl on the table and casually tossing it from one hand to the other before holding it up for her to examine. "It's round or to be more accurate, spherical; its reddish in color and it has", he sniffed it, "a fruity smell. No doubt if I were to bite into it, I would find it juicy and sweet.

"Now all of these – round, red, fruity, juicy, sweet – are adjectives describing the noun 'apple.' Or, to use more Advaitic terms, let me say that the 'apple' is the 'substantive' – the apparently real, separately existing thing – and all of the other words are 'attributes' of the apple – merely incidental qualities of the thing itself. Are you with me so far?"

She nodded hesitantly but, after a little reflection, more positively.

"But suppose I had carried out this analysis with the rose that we looked at a moment ago. I could have said that it was red, delicate, fragrant, thorny and so on. And we would have noted that all of those were simply attributes and that the actual existent thing, the substantive, was the rose. But then we went on to see that the rose wasn't real at all. It was just an assemblage of petals and sepals and so on – I'm afraid I am not a botanist! In the same way, we could say that the apple consists of seeds and flesh and skin. We may not be able to put these things together into any form different from an apple but Nature can.

"If you ask a scientist what makes an apple an apple, he will probably tell you that is the particular configuration of nucleotides in the DNA or RNA of the cells. There are many different species of apple and each one will have a slight variation in the chromosomes and it is that which differentiates the species. If you want to explain to someone what the difference is between a Bramley and a Granny Smith, you will probably say something like 'the Bramley is large and green, used mainly for cooking and is quite sharp tasting, while the

Granny Smith is still green but normally much smaller and sweeter'. But these are all adjectives or attributes. What is actually different is the physical makeup of the cell nuclei.

"But, if we look at a chromosome or a strand of DNA, are we actually looking at a self-existent, separate thing? If you look very closely through an electron microscope, you find that DNA is made up of four basic units arranged in pairs in a long, spiral chain. And any one of these units is itself made up of atoms of carbon, hydrogen, oxygen and nitrogen, again arranged in a very specific way. So even those are not separate 'things-in-themselves'; they are names given to particular forms of other, more fundamental things.

"And so we arrive at atoms – even the ancient Greeks used to think that everything was made up of atoms. Are these the final 'substantives' with all of the apparent things in the world being merely attributes? Well, unfortunately not. Science has known for a long time that atoms mainly consist of empty space with electrons spinning around a central nucleus of protons and neutrons. And science has known for somewhat less time that these particles, which were once thought to be fundamental, are themselves not solid, self-existent things but are either made up of still smaller particles or are in the form of waves, merely having probabilities of existence at many different points in space.

"Still more recently, science claimed that all of the different particles are themselves made out of different combinations of just a few particles called quarks and that those are the ultimately existing things. But they have not yet progressed far enough. The simple fact of the matter is that every 'thing' is ultimately only an attribute, a name and form superimposed upon a more fundamental substantive. We make the mistake of thinking that there really is a table, when actually there is only wood. We make the mistake of thinking that there is really wood, when actually there is only cellulose and sugars and proteins. We make the mistake of thinking there is protein when this is only a particular combination of atoms. "Ultimately, everything in the universe is seen to be only name and form of a single substantive.

The journalist was transfixed; not exactly open-mouthed but her pencil had not moved for some time. Eventually, she asked in a small voice: "But then where do I fit into all of this?"

"Ah", he replied. "That again depends upon what you mean by the word 'I'. Who you think you are – 'Sarah' – is essentially no different from the table and chair. You are simply name and form, imposed upon the non-dual reality. Who you really are, however… well, that is quite different – you are that non-dual reality. You see, in the final analysis, there are not two things; there is only non-duality. That is the truth; that is Advaita."

In these examples, then, each object that is initially thought to be separate is subsequently discovered to have only a 'dependent' reality. The table is really only a form of wood; the wood is really only a form of cellulose, which is a particular molecular configuration of carbon, hydrogen and oxygen and so on. Everything in the universe (and the universe itself) only has 'dependent' reality; nothing is 'real in itself'. There is no word in the English language to describe this concept so we are forced to resort to the Sanskrit term. The word for something (anything) that is not real in itself is 'mithya'. Our English word 'myth' probably derives from this, though the meaning is not quite the same.

But of course tables and people are not 'unreal'. Although they are not 'real in themselves', something about them is unquestionably real; something 'exists'. This ultimate reality is called Brahman in Advaita. We often refer to it as 'Consciousness' in English. It is also that which we ultimately are. The body and mind are only transient forms - mithya;

Consciousness is eternal - the only reality.

Another way of looking at this is that we effectively create the problem ourselves, through our habitual practice of 'naming'. A trivial example might be deciding to refer to a part of the earth that is higher than the surrounding land as a 'mountain'. Clearly this is very useful when we want to give directions to someone but the very naming seems to bring something 'separate' into existence and, in reality, this is not so. Another common example used in Advaita is the 'wave' and 'ocean'. We call the local bit that washes over our toes on the beach a 'wave' and the great mass that separates continents an 'ocean' but both are only ever water. Even a raindrop is the same water en route from ocean back to ocean via clouds and rivers. And the body of a person is only a mixture of organic and inorganic chemicals in the process of going from dust to dust, via food and living tissue.

The classic example used in the scripture is that of gold and ornaments - rings, necklaces and bangles. There is actually no such thing as a 'ring' - it is only a name we give to that particular form of gold. If you don't believe me, you keep the ring and just give me the gold! Another scriptural example is that of pots made out of clay. Of course the pot has utility from the empirical stand-point. It can hold your hot coffee conveniently while you wait for it to cool down sufficiently to drink. A lump of clay would obviously not be much help with this. But even so, the pot was clay before it was made into the form of a pot; it will be clay after it has broken and been thrown away and it is nothing other than clay even now. 'Pot' is only a 'name' that we give to that particular 'form; of clay - we could just as easily have made a flat disc and called it a 'plate'. 'Pot' as a separate thing has no reality - it is mithya. Similarly, everything is brahman and hence reality; but seeing and naming anything (as separate) is mithyA.

In these examples, then, all the various pots are mithya; the clay itself is the reality, satyam. Rings, bangles and bracelets are mithya; the gold is satyam. The world and everything and everyone in it are mithya; brahman is satyam. Mithya is transient, dependent, name and form only; satyam is eternal, independent, formless reality.

Adhyasa

There is really only one problem in life, as far as Advaita is concerned and that is that we fail to see things as they really are. We believe, erroneously, that we are each a separate person, living in a world of separate objects (that are usually out to get us!) Advaita tells us, in contradiction to our perception and upbringing (and also our 'common sense') that there is no separate world or other people. It tells us that we are confusing real and apparent, believing that we are limited when we are in fact unlimited. Our entire aim in life, even if we do not realize it, is to rid ourselves of these perceived limitations and 'become' unlimited. (Of course we cannot really become unlimited because we already are! What we actually want, if we only knew it, is to gain the *knowledge* that we are already unlimited.) This confusion or 'mixing up' of real and mithya, 'superimposing' something that is mithya upon the non-dual reality, is the reason why we find ourselves in this unhappy state of believing ourselves to be limited and incomplete, wanting to achieve some spurious completion by acquiring possessions or status.

There is a classic metaphor for this in the tradition of Advaita: that of the rope and the snake. In partial darkness, where we are unable to see clearly, we come upon a coiled-up rope and mistake it for a snake. As a result, we experience all of the symptoms that we would have if it were a real snake - sweating, anxiety and so on. If we bring a torch to shine upon the presumed snake, we realize that it is only a rope and all of our worries were unwarranted.

Here, the snake has no reality whatsoever - it is only an image conjured from our memory and superimposed upon the rope. We confuse or mix up the real rope and the unreal snake and suffer the consequences. The reason for the mistake is our partial ignorance. In total darkness, we would see nothing and there would be no problem. In sunlight, we would recognize the rope instantly and, again, there would be no problem. It is the mixture of partial knowledge (there is 'something' there) and partial ignorance (I don't know what it is) that brings about our fear.

Similarly, as regards the world, other objects or even ourselves, we have partial ignorance. I know that there is something - and I call it 'world', for example - but I don't really know what it is. I confuse the real Brahman with the mithya world and suffer the consequences.

This unintentional action of 'mixing up' or confusing what is real and what is mithya is called 'adhyasa'. Again, there is no equivalent word in English but it is one of the most important terms in Advaita. So you will have to learn the Sanskrit!

Adhyasa itself is not the same as 'ignorance', rather it arises as a result of ignorance. We believe we see a snake because our mind conjures up this image when the ambient light prevent us from seeing clearly. We think we are a limited individual in an essentially hostile world because our self-ignorance leads us to think that we are the mind and body, rather than the Consciousness that is temporarily enlivening the mind and body.

The process of discovering our way of looking at things to be mistaken, and realizing the 'actual' state of affairs, is called 'sublation'. At one point, I think that the object on the ground in front of me is a snake and act accordingly - ensure I have my phone with me so that I can call for an ambulance; look around for a large stick and so on. Upon tentatively moving closer, maybe throwing a stone at it, I suddenly realize that it is only a rope. The 'snake' is immediately sublated and I walk on past the rope without further concern.

Similarly, Advaita provides the Self-knowledge which enables me to realize that the world is only brahman and that I am brahman. There is no duality and no need to have any concerns about 'my life' or 'my death'.

'Levels of Reality'

The objective of Advaita is to educate us out of accepting the apparent world around us as the reality; to make us realize that all of this is only seeming name and form of a reality that is non-dual. But, given that we begin by firmly believing that the world is real, Advaita has to begin its teaching from this level of (mis)understanding. The empirical world is called vyavahara, which literally means 'action, practice or doing'; it is the world of 'transactions'. (There is also the level of dream or imagination, in which any transactions are unreal. We may see a unicorn in our dream but, on waking, we acknowledge that such a thing does not really exist - this level of 'reality' [or 'unreality'] is called pratibhasa. It is mentioned for completeness and you can now forget about it!)

Absolute reality is called paramartha, and here there can be no transactions because there is no doer, doing, or any object to be affected. A famous prayer in the scriptures asks the Lord to 'Lead us from the unreal to the real; from darkness into light; from death to immortality'. Enlightenment is the paradigm leap of understanding that brings this about.

But there is clearly much scope for confusion here! Whenever a statement is made in Advaita, we have to ask whether the statement is being made from the empirical level of vyavahara, or (as if) from the level of absolute reality, paramartha.(You have to be careful here because, of course, you cannot actually make any statement in paramartha because the reality is non-dual.) Many Western teachers mix up these levels, because they do not acknowledge the distinction, so that it is hardly surprising that many seekers in the West do not really understand Advaita!

So, what ultimately is real? Well, we have established that the objects in the world (and the world itself) are mithya – they have only dependent realty. Any given thing is only name and form of something more fundamental. It could also be thought of as depending upon me, the knower. For a thing to be said to 'exist', it has to be an object of knowledge. And an object of knowledge has to have a 'knower' so that it can be 'known'. It must be observed, or inferred - if not by me, then by someone else, or at least by some entity which is conscious of the thing. And if not at this point in time, at least in the past or future. If no one had ever been aware of X at any time, and never would be for the rest of eternity, how could X be said to exist? It would not, and could never, be known. The known depends upon the knower for its existence.

Furthermore, in order for me to become the 'knower' of an object, I have to choose to use the appropriate means of knowledge (see next chapter) and direct my conscious awareness. For example, in order to 'know' the person who has just come into the room, my eyes have to be opened, pointed in the right direction and focused, and my brain has to be linked in to process the data, cross-reference to memory and so on. All this is only possible as a result of Consciousness. Therefore, the 'knower' function is dependent upon Consciousness.

The 'known' is dependent upon the 'knower' and the 'knower' is dependent upon 'I', the Consciousness principle. Consciousness is the only thing, ultimately, that is not dependent upon anything. Being dependent equates to mithya. Therefore the only reality is Consciousness.

Maya

So why does there appear to be a world then, you might ask.

Much of Advaita is concerned with providing explanations at the empirical level of vyavahara. We know (or will do by the time you finish the book) that such explanations are inevitably mithya also, because reality is non-dual - so there is no world, no person to see it etc. But, until such time as we realize this (become enlightened), interim explanations are needed. And this is where the magical force of maya is brought in.

Maya is the name given to the 'force' or 'principle' which causes us to see a world of duality when the reality is non-dual. It is key to Shankara's presentation of the philosophy. The word itself can mean 'illusion', 'unreality' or even 'witchcraft' and 'magic'. It is said to have two aspects. From the universal level, there is a 'projecting' power called vikshepa, which produces the world of plurality like a film on a cinema screen. At the individual level, there is a veiling power called avarana, which brings about the ignorance that prevents us from seeing the truth. This individual ignorance is called avidya. So the usual way that Advaita speaks about this subject is to refer to maya, meaning the projecting power, when referring to the 'illusion' of creation. And we refer to avidya when talking about the individual's ignorance resulting from the veiling power.

In reality, there is only name and form of the non-dual Brahman; the appearance of the world is just that - an appearance. Maya is mithya. But the world is still empirically real. Even once you have appreciated the truth of all this, the world-appearance will continue; just as, knowing that the earth goes around the sun, you still see the sunrise and sunset and make use of these 'events' in your day-to-day life.

4

Why is Self-knowledge so important?

One of the ten most famous Upanishads (Mundaka 1.1.3) asks the question: What is that one thing which, once we know it, we effectively know everything? On the face of it, this might appear to be like the Zen koans which present mind-bending questions that have no answer. But Advaita does not go in for this sort of thing and we are later told (2.2.12) that 'all this (world) is Brahman alone'. And Brahman is (1.1.6) 'that which is not the object of sense perception, unborn, does not have any attributes, is eternal and all-pervasive, and is the cause of all beings'. And the Chandogya Upanishad, in the single most important statement in the whole of Advaita states that 'You are That'.

These astonishing facts, if facts they are, cannot be gleaned from any other source. If it is true that 'I am Brahman, which is the only reality', then this must be true NOW. (Advaita effectively defines truth as that knowledge which can never be contradicted.) Yet we do not know this, despite everything that we have perceived in our lifetime and reasoned from that. But this does not mean that we cannot know it.

Suppose that you and a friend, A, both went to school with a third person, X. Although you were not particularly friendly with X, you knew him quite well but, since leaving school you lost touch and have forgotten all about him. Today, you happen to be walking along with A and see Y, who is a famous film star, walking by on the other side of the street. You have seen films starring Y and admire him very much. A now makes some comment such as "Y has come a long way in the world since we knew him, hasn't he?" You are mystified since you have never even spoken to Y as far as you know and you ask A to explain himself. A then makes the revelatory statement: 'Y is that X whom we knew at school.'

All of the contradictory aspects, that X is an insignificant, scruffy, spotty oik that you once knew at school, while Y is a rich, famous and talented actor, are all cancelled out, leaving the bare equation that X and Y are the same person. Furthermore, the knowledge is immediate. We do not have to go over the reasoning or meditate upon it for a long time.

In the same way, if we learn all about advaita with the help of a qualified teacher who understands the scriptures, this is equivalent to getting to know X. Then comes the time when we hear the words 'You are X' and the sudden realization may then dawn that this is all true.

We normally consider that we begin life in a state of ignorance and that we subsequently undergo a process of education, from one source or another, acquiring the knowledge that we are told we need in order to function in life. We observe the world around us and gradually build up an understanding about it, with or without the help of parents and teachers.

Indian philosophies have divided the 'means' by which we acquire knowledge into a number of categories and the three main ones are as follows:

- Perception - Information obtained via the five sense organs; e.g. you are currently seeing this book in front of you.
- Inference - The classical example is that, in the past you have previously observed that, whenever you encounter smoke, there is invariably something burning. Therefore, when you see smoke on the top of a distant hill, you infer that there must be a fire.
- Testimony - When you are unable to verify something directly for yourself, it is usual to accept the word of someone trustworthy, whether this is a friend telling you

that a mutual acquaintance has just got married or a newspaper telling you that a volcano has just erupted on the other side of the world.

All of the knowledge that we acquire relates to things (some of which may be 'subtle', of course, such as concepts). And, as we have just seen in the last chapter, 'things' are mithya. So all that we say we know refers to attributes only and not to the essential reality. Indeed, we can only perceive, think or speak about categories, attributes, actions or relationships. Since the essential reality has none of these, we cannot speak about it directly at all.

Furthermore, worldly knowledge always involves a subject 'I' knowing something about an object, which is different from me. Self-knowledge is not like this, because subject and object are the same. So the usual means for obtaining knowledge are of no use. This is why science can never tell us anything about the nature of consciousness.

So how, then, may we gain any knowledge at all about the 'essential reality'? Well, it has already been argued in the last chapter that this reality is, in fact, the Consciousness that we are. So, in a sense, nothing could be easier to discover, since I am that realty.

Or so it would seem... Unfortunately, there is this minor problem of our being ignorant of this truth and, instead, super-imposing some mistaken view of who-I-am - such as 'I am this body, which is born and is going to die'. Accordingly, what is needed is for someone who has seen through this confusion and directly understood the true nature of reality to explain things to us in a reasonable and logical manner so that we can finally see it for ourselves.

And it is why Vedanta *can* reveal this knowledge, by acting as a 'mirror' in which we may recognize the 'reflection' of ourselves. This is an aspect of 'testimony'. There is a famous story which illustrates this need for a teacher or guru:

Ten men cross a river in flood and lose their footing. They swim to the other bank and re-assemble. When they count the number of survivors, they find only nine and lament the loss of one. A passing monk hears their story and realizes their mistake. He touches each man, counting out the number, and thus demonstrates that all ten are present. Each man, when counting the others, had forgotten to count himself. Similarly, we each forget our true self until this is pointed out by the teacher. In the context of the story, as the monk touches the last man and says 'you are the tenth', direct knowledge arises.

Initially, we will object strongly to all of these ideas - after all, we can see the snake and we know that it is a poisonous one! Accordingly, we should ideally find someone in whose integrity we have complete trust; someone with whom we can temporarily suspend our current beliefs, and to whom we can listen with an open mind. Such a person is called a 'guru'. In the absence of access to a guru (and there are not many of them around in the West who are genuinely qualified - see the chapter on 'Teaching'), we have to rely upon written material. And the final authority is the scripture mentioned in the first chapter.

And this is where that much-maligned word 'faith' enters the equation. Suppose that you are told something by a friend, whose word you trust completely, but you are unable to verify this for yourself. You do not doubt the friend's honesty or sincerity. At the worst, you might think that he has himself been misled. In the case of the scriptures of Vedanta, the truth of these has been validated time and again by sages over several thousand years.

So, less emotive than the word 'faith', we could say 'trust' in the teachers and 'respect' for the scriptures and the proven value of these over the ages. Until such time as we realize the truth for ourselves, we have to trust that those who have gone before, who were in the same situation as ourselves and who did succeed in dispelling their ignorance, are being honest with us. Note that this is not to say that we have to dispense with reason. On the contrary, we are never asked to accept anything that is contrary to reason or to our own experience. We are asked to put aside temporarily our convictions about what we think we already know, however, and to look afresh at ourselves and the world around us in the light of these new ideas that are being presented.

This is quite unlike most religions where, for example, we are asked to accept the existence of a heaven and hell which can never be validated until after we have died! With Advaita, it is perfectly possible to realize the truth for ourselves in this lifetime - many have done so. The truth is that you are already perfect, complete and without limitations of any kind - even though you do not know this, and are almost certainly quite disinclined to believe it!

5

Am I only this body and mind?

As has been noted, our natural tendency from a very early age is to believe that we are this physical body, from whose portals we seem to peer. It is understandable why this should be, of course: we see through the eyes and, when we close the eyes, the vision disappears. We feel things by reaching out with the hands and touching them. All of our senses tell us that, if we are not literally the body, then at least we are 'contained' within it. And such an idea is reinforced by everyone with whom we come into contact - because they have also come to accept this in the same way.

And even if we accept intellectually that we cannot be the physical body, since we know that the body that we have in old age is vastly different from that we had as a baby, we are likely still to believe that we are the mind. And we probably believe that the mind is an a aspect of the physical brain. After all, we know that the behavior and mental abilities of someone who has been brain damaged change dramatically. Indeed, we may feel that a relative who develops Alzheimer's disease, for example, effectively becomes a different person.

Religions may tell us that who-we-really-are is an immortal 'soul' that is only temporarily housed inside this mortal body; that we are destined for a heaven or a hell, dependent upon our conviction in these beliefs and the extent to which we abide by their rules. But, for most people, this remains a feeble hope rather than certain knowledge. And perhaps the majority feels that their existence and associated awareness will terminate with the death of this current body. But Advaita tells us that we are actually the 'Consciousness' by whose 'light' the material body and the subtle mind are able to function.

At a level beyond the merely physical, we often tend to identify with the roles that we play. Thus, for example, some might claim 'I am a banker' (or maybe they would only admit this under duress...) Or, in the family context, one might say 'I am a mother'. But the very fact that these are contextual shows that one cannot actually 'be' such things. Even if you are very attached to the job that you do, and it means far more than simply earning money, you will not cease to exist when you retire. And, though you might be a 'mother' to your children, you will also necessarily be a 'daughter' to your parents and probably a 'wife' to your husband.

This tendency to 'identify' with something in the apparent creation is associated with a particular aspect of the mind in Advaita. It is called 'ahankara' and the dictionary definition of this Sanskrit term is 'the making of the self'. It means, simply, saying 'I am X' or 'I am Y' and truly believing this; i.e. identifying with something else and thereby erroneously defining who you are. It can be equated with the ego in Western terminology and it is not who you really are. You are neither the body, nor mind, nor the ego. You are not even a person. Rather you should think of this last term as the 'persona' - a false mask that is adopted by someone to present to the outside world.

Much of the teaching of Advaita is concerned with ridding you of these false notions and one of the most famous instructions, from one of the Upanishads, tells you to bring to mind the phrase 'neti, neti', which means 'not this, not this', whenever we find ourselves in this wrong frame of mind.

Basically, Consciousness is not amenable to language or thought at all. All that we can describe or think about are objects of our perception or thought. But Consciousness cannot ever be objectified; it is that which enables us to perceive or think; it is the ultimate subject. Everything else is mithya, dependent upon Consciousness, which is the only reality. But then I do not need to perceive it or think about it - because I am That. As a knower, I am mithya but, as that which enables the knowing to take place, I am satyam, the reality.

6

Who am I?

This is the most difficult chapter, so make sure you are fully awake before starting!

Jivas

In this world that we see around us, there appears to be people separate from ourselves. Much of our life is concerned with interacting with these 'others', at both physical and mental levels. It seems indisputable that my body is different from yours and, although we may find it difficult to define exactly what we mean by 'mind', it seems to be equally indisputable that we do not know what others are thinking or feeling.

People are born, grow old and eventually die. Whether they are subsequently reborn in different bodies is something you may well doubt but the (reasonable) principles behind karma and reincarnation have already been discussed in the chapter on Action. Advaita refers to the 'jiva', which 'inhabits' the body and transmigrates after death. (Note that *all* living beings, including plants, 'contain' a jiva, or perhaps more accurately 'are' jivas.)

According to Advaita, the process of rebirth will continue until such time as knowledge is gained of the true nature of the Self. When speaking of an 'individual', his or her 'real self' is called the Atman. For a human being, there is the possibility of realizing the truth of this. Unfortunately, the mind has this natural tendency to identify this 'I' with the inert material body, mind and roles etc as described in the previous chapter. When I say that 'I am conscious' and 'I exist', the 'I' is the Atman, although the thought itself is associated with the mind and brain of an individual person. The person will die, but 'I' will not.

And, as already stated at the beginning of this book, the Atman is Brahman. So the corollary, of the above, lest you should still have any doubt, is that my 'I' and your 'I' – indeed the 'I' of everything – is the same. Indeed, there is only 'I', taking the name and form of everything.

Ishvara

When I dream, my mind conjures up an entire world, replete with mountains and cities, and people seemingly going about their own business. For the duration of the dream, all seems as real as the waking world. Clearly, I (the jiva) do not conjure up the 'real' world in the same way. Advaita attributes this function to Ishvara, who manifests as the entire world of duality, which duality has for its actual being the non-dual reality, Brahman. Ishvara wields the power of maya, as described earlier, to bring about the world-illusion.

Just as the world, together with its myriad life-forms and apparently separate objects, is accorded an empirical reality, so also are the many gods who are said to control the functioning of the universe. Thus, there are gods for the sun and moon, for the wind and fire, for knowledge and prosperity. The idea behind this is that, whatever we may be doing, going about our daily business or personal pursuits, we may acknowledge the existence of a higher principle, representing the truth behind the appearance. Thus, it is said, there are many gods but only one God in Hinduism. Each is an aspect of Ishvara, who ultimately controls the whole show. Note that this is not to say that the gods are imaginary; a merely fanciful idea, part of a complex religious system built up from an original, unscientific ignorance. The gods have as much reality as do the jivas. But, in the final analysis, they too are also mithya.

Brahman

Referring to the metaphor of wave and ocean etc, the name given to water, as opposed to wave or ocean, is Brahman. Brahman is the 'bottom line'; the only reality, eternal and unlimited. Every-seeming-thing is only name and form of Brahman.

Who am I?

Most readers will have heard of Ramana Maharshi, who was teaching in the 1930s. He has come to be known especially for his 'method' of advocating that seekers conduct self enquiry by repeatedly asking the question 'who am I?' I would argue that this should not be taken literally – simply asking that question without the guidance of scriptures or a teacher is unlikely to lead anywhere. But the answer to the question, when it finally arrives, is the answer to everything! Because, of course 'I' am everything!

And this last statement is the sort of statement that causes so much confusion when people encounter Advaita. We have already looked in the last chapter at how we identify with our body, mind, and the roles that we play in our lives. One of the teaching practices in Advaita looks at the three different states of experience the mind passes through every day: waking, dreaming and deep-sleep. In the West, we regard ourselves as the 'waking person'. We acknowledge that there is a dream state in which all sorts of unusual things happen but we believe that these are all simply a product of a mind that is not currently being controlled by an 'I'. And, of course, there is a deep sleep state but here we think that the 'I' is totally absent.

But Advaita's take on this is quite different. Who we really are is the Atman. In the waking state, consciousness is directed to the (gross) outside world and 'I' is taken to be the body, which is a part of that world. In dream, the mind generates its own (subtle) world and a new imaginary body. We now identify the Atman with this dream world and body. In the deep sleep state, it is not that the 'I' is absent (although the 'I thought' is absent!), but rather that there are neither gross nor subtle objects. Accordingly, we are aware of nothing and there is no mind active to identify the Atman with anything.

So Advaita says that we are not the waker, the dreamer or the deep-sleeper - we are the ever-present, witnessing Atman which is 'behind' all of these; the Atman who 'lights up' the experiences of waking and dreaming, and the 'non-experience' (or rather 'experience of nothing') of deep sleep.

In fact, Advaita recognizes 5 'states' of consciousness: waking, dreaming, sleeping, unconsciousness and death. (NB. Not 5 states of Atman – Atman has no states! The mind experiences the changing states but the Atman is changeless.) Each state of experience has its own special characteristics, which means that each has to be regarded as unique. Consciousness is directed outwards through the senses and organs of action to the gross world in the waking state. It is directed inwards to the mind in the dream state, when that mind creates its own subtle world. And it is unmanifest in the deep sleep state, when 'I know nothing'.

Reflected Consciousness

But there is a problem with this explanation. If as Advaita says, there is only Consciousness, how is it that I see only out of my eyes in the waking state, and only see the content of my dreams in the dream state? The answer to this is explained by the metaphor of a mirror. The 'consciousness' that is doing my seeing during waking and dream states is only 'reflected' consciousness. The Atman itself is not a seer, doer, enjoyer etc. at all.

Suppose that we have a dark, shuttered room. It is so dark that we are unable to find anything inside it. We are only able to open the door and, although there is bright sunlight outside, this does not penetrate far enough to illumine the interior. There is no electricity and I do not have a torch. I do, however, have a mirror. By positioning myself in the doorway, I can hold the mirror at such an angle that the sunlight reflects in the mirror and illumines the contents of the room. Although the mirror is itself inert, having no light of its own, it becomes a source of light by virtue of reflecting the light from the sun, which does have its own light. This, of course, is also how we get the moonlight by which we can see during the night, when there is a moon in a cloudless sky. The light of the moon is simply the reflected light of the sun.

The parallel can now be made with our own inert equipments and Consciousness. Brahman is the equivalent of the sun, the only true 'source' of Consciousness. Brahman 'illumines' the instrument of the mind, which itself is not a source of Consciousness. But, by virtue of this illumination, the mind is able to reflect the Consciousness via the senses into the 'room' of the world and become aware of the objects therein and interact with them (including the body-mind itself). It is the mind that 'knows', not the Atman. The Atman is that by which everything is known, just as the sun is that by which everything is seen – the sun itself does not see.

Furthermore, when we see an object, we register the object itself (i.e. its name, form and attributes) but rarely think that this is only possible because light is being reflected off it from an external source. Similarly, in respect of our actual awareness of objects or of our own body and mind, we register that we are aware of something but not that by which we are aware, i.e. the Atman itself. Once I have acknowledged that my feeling of being an aware, conscious being is because Consciousness is reflecting in my (independently) inert mind, I can also acknowledge that it is the same Consciousness reflecting in other independently inert minds that gives the impression of other people.

The jiva is the reflection of Consciousness in a particular body-mind. Each person is therefore different, being dependent on that particular body-mind (which derives from the karmas of past lives), just as the way the sun gets reflected in a mirror is dependent upon the nature of the mirror. A dirty mirror will result in an unclear reflection; a distorting mirror will give a distorted image and so on. The 'original Consciousness' is totally unaffected, just as the sun is unaffected by the character of its reflection. The 'original Consciousness' (Brahman) is not a doer or enjoyer. It is subtler than space, which is everywhere, unaffected by the movement of the objects within it.

Accordingly, to come back to Ramana Maharshi's 'Who am I?', we start off by believing we are the ego but in the end we realize that I am Consciousness itself, whose reflection is 'lighting up' the otherwise inert mind. At the empirical level of appearance (vyavahAra) we are separate individuals but at the level of absolute reality (paramArtha), we are Consciousness or Brahman itself. Without the Consciousness, the mind is inert. Whilst we remain identified with the reflection, we continue to believe that we are mortal and limited because we believe our existence is dependent upon the body/mind. As soon as we realize ourselves to be the original, we recognize that we are eternal and forever free. And as long as we mix up the two, we remain confused!

The scriptures tell us that the Self does not act. This would seem quite inexplicable on the face of it but, following on from the above explanation, it can now be understood this statement is true - from the standpoint of absolute reality. But, at the empirical level, there is nothing else that can initiate action other than Consciousness. It is this 'reflected Consciousness', operating through the instrument of the mind that effectively acts, i.e. the 'I' that we normally assume ourselves to be. So we can say that I am both a 'doer' and an 'enjoyer' of action from the empirical standpoint. But I am neither a doer nor an enjoyer from the standpoint of absolute reality. To put this in the sort of way that the Upanishads tend to explain things: Consciousness is not a 'doer', but there is no doer other than Consciousness, in the same way that water is not a wave but the wave is nothing other than water.

And one final point to note again, if you have followed the above explanation is this: reality is non-dual, so it makes no sense to talk of a 'Consciousness' *and* a 'reflected Consciousness'! So you must always bear in mind (sorry to keep repeating this but it is very important) that all of these explanations are interim only, to bring about Self-knowledge. In the end they are mithya. It is like the pole that you use to raise your body to the level of the bar in pole-vaulting. If you are to clear the jump, you have to let go of the pole!

7

Has the universe been created?

Creation

Religions, together with those philosophies that accept the existence of a god, usually claim that God is the creator of the universe. When they use this word 'creation', however, what they invariably mean is that God is the intelligent cause of the universe. Indeed, probably the most commonly used argument for God is the argument from design and the metaphor often encountered is the one of the watchmaker.

When we look at the internal mechanism of a watch, it is said, the workings are so complex that it is inconceivable that they could have come together accidentally - there must be an intelligent designer. In the same way, then, since the world around us exhibits so much complexity and yet all of the various functions operate together with beauty and efficiency, there must be an intelligence behind its creation.

Philosophy differentiates the 'intelligent cause' as described here from the 'material cause'. As an example a wooden table or chair has, as its intelligent cause, a carpenter (ignoring the complications of modern self-assembly furniture). But the material cause of both (table and chair, that is - not carpenter) is wood. Advaita is unique amongst philosophies in claiming that God (or more pedantically Ishvara) is the material cause as well as the intelligent cause. This follows from the earlier discussions on 'mithya', since we have seen that everything has Brahman (i.e. Ishvara from the perspective of vyavahara) as its ultimate substrate or dependent reality.

Of course, if you are really alert, you might at this point be asking how there can be a creation at all, since this seems to contradict the very basis of the statement made by Advaita that 'there are not two things'. And you would be right to do so! Hopefully, this chapter will resolve such issues!

Attribution and rescission

First of all, it is necessary to mention one of the fundamental aspects in the teaching of advaita, namely the practice of stating something as true and then later modifying it - attribution and rescission or retraction. The technical term for this is 'adhyaropa – apavada'. What it means in essence is that what you're told initially may not actually be completely true! It is the intention of the teacher to address a seeker at his or her present level of understanding. By analogy, if you think of someone learning mathematics, there would be little point in teaching differential calculus to a student who has yet to learn algebra, and algebra would be of little value to someone who did not even know basic arithmetic.

Note that this does *not* mean that you cannot trust what the teacher tells you! In fact, many teachers will give you the bottom line right from the start, even though you will almost certainly not understand why it is so. What they will then do, however, is start from the beginning, using simple arithmetic! There is no point in being impatient. You have to take it step by step. Indeed, patience is one of the mental prerequisites for studying Advaita.

For example, there are several accounts in the Upanishads of how the world was created by God. Typically, these involve progressive creation from the basic elements but the various stories differ widely in detail. The skeptic can easily use this as an argument for pointing out the inconsistency in the scriptures. But they are not meant to be taken literally. At a simplistic level, they may be viewed in much the same way as one might tell a young child that she was 'brought by the storks', rather than attempting a description of the process of conception, growth in the womb and birth. It satisfies for the time being until she is ready for a more sophisticated explanation.

Differing theories of creation

To continue, then, with the developing explanation of creation: Because Advaita utilizes this methodology of providing explanations appropriate to the level of understanding of the student, it is also natural that it should make use of theories provided by other schools of philosophy. And so it does! The next major explanation to be presented is that used by the Sankhya philosophers. It is called 'satkarya vada' and this means the theory (vada) that the effect (karya) is already existent (sat). More usually, it is said that the effect already exists in the cause and the metaphor that is often used to explain this is that of the sculptures of Michelangelo. It is said that he used to claim that he did not really create his sculptures; rather he chiseled away the marble to reveal what was already there beneath.

This is how Sankhya (and Yoga) philosophers envisaged creation and another name they used was 'transformation'. The unmanifest nature was 'transformed' into the people and objects that we see in the world around us.

Two other schools, the Nyaya and Vaisheshika philosophies held the opposite view, namely that an effect was not pre-existing in the cause but created anew by the efficient cause (e.g. Michelangelo). And Advaita (eventually) shows how each of these theories successfully contradicts the other and that neither is therefore tenable. The first is tantamount to saying that something that already exists can be born. The second effectively says that something can come out of nothing. For example, chipping away the marble might reveal a fully functioning Aston Martin instead. (And this argument applies equally to the Big Bang theory, of course. How could the creation come out of nothing? It would, at the very least, contradict the Law of Conservation of mass-energy.)

This analysis leads on to the more sophisticated explanation of what is called vivarta vada - the theory that the effect is only an apparent transformation. The argument is that the confusion arises because of language. We give something a name for convenience and, as a result of constant use, we take it for granted that the word refers to some separately existing thing. The classic examples that are quoted in the scriptures are clay-pot and gold-ring-bangle etc. When the potter makes a pot out of a lump of clay, the resultant object clearly has a new function. It can hold a liquid so that we can use it as a drinking vessel, for example. But we quickly forget that the pot is not a new thing in its own right. In the beginning, it was simply a lump of clay. Now, it is clay shaped into a more useful form. If we break it, it will still be clay, albeit now in pieces with little use of their own. It is never anything other than clay.

Problem of language

The Chandogya Upanishad (6.1.4 - 6) says that any product is only a new word: "just as, through a single clod of clay, all that is made of clay would become known, for all modification is but name based upon words and the clay alone is real..." And the same argument applies to everything. Any given object, as we learned earlier is only mithya; its reality is always only Brahman. Its seeming difference depends ultimately on mere words. The making of the pot is simply changing the form of the clay and giving it a new name.

In the same way, then, when the world and the jiva come into being, all that is happening is that Brahman is acquiring new forms and new names to go with them. But, before, during and after, all that actually exists is Brahman.

No creation

And that brings us to the ultimate explanation for creation, when all of the earlier, provisional theories have been rescinded. This is simply that there has never been any creation at all. This is called ajati vada - the 'unborn' theory. If the world can neither exist nor not-exist prior to creation, the only logical conclusion is that there has not been any creation at all. This is the contention of Gaudapada, supposed to have been the teacher of Shankara's guru. The theory is called ajati vada (ajati means 'not born'). The world has always existed because effectively there is no world – there is only name and form of the non-dual Brahman. Gaudapada, in his explanatory verses on one of the Upanishads, says: "No kind of jiva is ever born nor is there any cause for any such birth. The ultimate truth is that nothing whatsoever is born."

8

How do I become enlightened?

Many of the chapter headings in this book will not seem relevant to the person who is looking into all of this for the first time. He will have heard that there is this 'state' called enlightenment, and that it is desirable, and he will simply want to know what he has to do to get it.

The aim of any teaching of Advaita is to bring about enlightenment in the student, which begs the question of what exactly do we mean by enlightenment?

Most people who have not previously investigated non-dual teachings, and advaita in particular, will most likely have a distorted view, if not a totally wrong impression, about the meaning of the word 'enlightenment'. Their most likely source of 'knowledge' will be a popular magazine, film or work of fiction. And these invariably promote the idea that enlightenment is some sort of experience, evoked by heightened awareness, perhaps triggered by drugs. In fact enlightenment is not an experience at all. Experiences come and go, whereas enlightenment, once it occurs, is permanent. It is not a state of mind; there are no levels, so that it is neither high nor deep. It is binary - you are either enlightened or not. And, although drugs may distort mental perception, they will not bring enlightenment.

In fact, enlightenment equates to Self-knowledge. So what you have to do to begin with is understand and totally accept everything that you read in this book! When you directly recognize the truth of what is being pointed out, *that* is enlightenment.

'Paths' to realization

Someone who has a little more background may well have heard of up to 6 or 7 different so-called paths, which may be followed. Briefly, these are karma yoga or the path of action, bhakti yoga or the path of devotion, jnana yoga or the path of knowledge, raja or Royal Yoga (otherwise known as ashtanga yoga), Direct Path, Self Enquiry, Western-style satsang and Neo-advaita. I would like to say a little about each of these before expanding upon the correct, traditional approach to enlightenment. Note that these descriptions are necessarily very simplistic and, as with any of the topics in this book, you can find volumes written on each (although they may be in Sanskrit!) More will be said about some aspects of these in the last chapter.

- **Karma yoga** - this refers to the discipline of pursuing a life of selfless action, in accordance with dharma, as discussed in the chapter on Action.
- **Bhakti yoga** - this involves devotion to a personalized God, through dedication, sacrifice, prayer and worship.
- **Jnana yoga** - this is the process of learning about the nature of oneself from the scriptures as interpreted by a qualified teacher. This is effectively the subject of this book.
- **Raja yoga** - this incorporates a number of disciplines, as they were laid down by the sage Patanjali in the text called the 'Yoga Sutras of Patanjali'. This actually belongs to the philosophy of Yoga (which is a dualistic philosophy) and not Advaita but there is much overlap of the disciplines themselves and they were highly regarded by Shankara. Some of these will be outlined below.
- **Direct Path** - this is the philosophy as interpreted by the sage Atmananda Krishna Menon and attempts to bypass the need to understand the teachings of the scriptures and instead look directly to one's own experience and show that, when correctly analyzed, this leads to the realization that no dualism is involved.

49

- **Self Enquiry** - this is the process recommended by the modern sage Ramana Maharshi, who often told those seekers who came to him, repeatedly to ask themselves the question 'Who am I?', acknowledging that any answer presented by the mind was ultimately inadequate. In fact, there is no indication that he ever intended that this process in itself would lead to enlightenment. Rather, it should be considered as an element of jnana yoga itself.

- **Western-style satsang** – this is the term applied to most modern teachers in the West who travel around the world holding short meetings, and maybe weekend or week-long residential courses. They may begin be talking about some aspect of Advaita but mostly they simply answer random questions from the audience which, more often than not are about personal problems rather than general questions about the non-dual teaching.

- **Neo-advaita** - many modern Western teachers now claim that there can be no path at all, since there is no seeker to begin with! Unfortunately, though this may be ultimately true, it is of no help whatsoever to the ignorant seeker. Whilst the seeker takes himself to be a suffering individual, it is essential that he follow some effective path, ultimately to eliminate that ignorance.

In fact, traditional advaita could be thought to embody aspects of all of these, even neo-advaita (since there are some elements of correspondence with the teachings of Gaudapada, for example, although most neo-Advaitins are unlikely to be aware of this). As has already been seen, the theory of karma forms a fundamental element of the teaching. We have to act, and actions will necessarily incur consequences. And everything we do should be done in a spirit of reverence for the truth. Until we realize this for ourselves, there should be due reverence for the guru. This is the bhakti element. Jnana Yoga is, of course, the key to everything. In a sense, it is the only approach that will work; everything else is supplementary. Only knowledge can remove ignorance. In order to put the mind into a suitable state for it to be able to gain that knowledge, certain mental disciplines etc are needed. This is where Raja Yoga comes in. Traditional teaching incorporates methods which look into our beliefs about who we are and reveal that we are not what we thought we were - here are elements of direct path and self enquiry. Finally, the scriptures reveal that there has never been any creation, there are no individuals in reality, and therefore it is meaningless to talk about such individuals becoming enlightened - 'I' am already free. But this message is not expected to be understood until the latter stages. Initially, we firmly believe ourselves to be separate persons and thus have to be treated as such.

What to do to gain enlightenment

One of the questions most frequently asked by seekers, understandably, is: "What do I have to do in order to gain enlightenment?" And the disconcerting answer that you would have to give them, if being totally honest, is that you cannot do anything. 'Doing' is all about changing something - getting from A to B; acquiring something that you currently do not have; creating, altering, achieving, executing and so on. A powerful metaphor explains why this is: A lady discovers that she has lost her necklace after returning from visiting a friend, to whom she had been showing the necklace. She realizes that she must have left it there and runs out into the street and all the way back to her friend's house only to have the friend point out that the necklace was around her neck the whole time. The interesting question is whether it was necessary for her to return to her friend in order to find the necklace?

Clearly she already had the necklace but, equally clearly, she did not know that she had it. And this is the key point of the metaphor. We are already free but we do not know it. The only purpose of any practice that we might do is to acquire the knowledge that will remove the notion that we are bound to begin with.

There is nothing that you can do to become what you already are, but there are things that you can do in order to recognize it. This is what 'enlightenment' means - 'lighting up' what was there all the time!

As will be discussed in the final chapter, enlightenment is said to occur when the ignorance about our true nature is replaced by knowledge. In order for this to be possible, it is necessary that the mind be in a suitably prepared state. A mind that is worrying, speculating, argumentative or in any other agitated state will be unable to understand or accept a teaching which contradicts our habitual way of looking at our lives. On the contrary, our mind must be still and open, able to see clearly and exercise discrimination. These and many other traits must be cultivated if the mind is to be suitably receptive to the teaching. Without them, seeking will be a waste of time.

The process of discovering our true nature can therefore effectively be divided into two aspects. Ultimately, we have to acquire that knowledge which will destroy our self-ignorance - there is no other way. But certain attitudes of mind and modes of behavior are conducive to this whilst others are not. We will look into these attitudes and disciplines first.

Preparation
Traditionally, there are two stages to this.

Karma Yoga
The first of these is usually called karma yoga, which may be thought of as 'right action'. Traditionally, actions are performed as an offering to the Lord and, most importantly, whatever happens is accepted as a 'gift' from the Lord. Of course we still act in order to obtain a specific result (otherwise we would never

get out of bed) but whatever the outcome, it is 'ok'.

More generally, one should be a good citizen and family member – have due respect for one's parents and society, devote part of one's time to helping within the community and giving assistance to others less fortunate than oneself etc. Even such things as 'living in an ecological sound manner', 'avoiding needless cruelty to animals', and so on are all relevant.

This is all common sense, really. It simply means behaving at all times in such a way as is morally responsible and considerate of others; in accordance with dharma. It is okay to pursue one's own desires, providing that these do not contravene the above considerations.

Karma yoga is essentially about modifying our behavior such that the first two goals of life mentioned in the chapter on action become of reducing importance, whilst the last two grow more dominant. Eventually, the overriding desire is to attain moksha or 'liberation'.

Upasana Yoga

The word 'upasana' literally means 'serving, waiting upon, service, attendance, respect' or ' homage, adoration, worship' but it is effectively used to refer to all of those aspects other than the acquiring of self-knowledge (jnana); i.e. to the preparation element dealt with by the first part of the Vedas, rather than the 'final stages' of the end portion (Vedanta). Basically, it is about acquiring the discipline that will enable the mind to take on board the message of Advaita.

At a simplistic level, this discipline encompasses all key aspects of the body and mind, maintaining a healthy lifestyle, with balanced work, rest and play and disciplining one's thoughts and actions, mind and senses. These latter aspects are encapsulated in what is known as the 'six-fold discipline', which forms the third stage of the 'four-fold qualification' specified in the scriptures. (Perhaps the simplest texts which speak of these are the Tattva Bodha, which is specifically addressed to the new seeker and the Vivekachudamani or 'Crest Jewel of Discrimination'.)

The breakdown of the **Fourfold Qualification** is as follows:

1. Discrimination

Advaita talks about a number of different aspects of this. There is discrimination between what is transient and what is eternal; between the observer and the object; between the self and the not-self. It is about making the right choice between alternatives, based on both reason and morality. Specifically, it means choosing what is ultimately 'good' rather than what is merely transiently 'pleasant'. It entails the realization that the changing aspects of life can never bring lasting happiness.

2. Dispassion

Right discrimination is really not possible without dispassion. Dispassion means 'without desire'; having neither lust nor loathing for worldly objects. It is the ability to stand back, see things as they are, not get involved and other such clichés. If we are attached to something, i.e. if we desire it rather than an alternative, then it is clearly difficult to discriminate. Discrimination implies reasoned impartiality. It does not mean that we have always to turn away from what is pleasant, which would simply be silly, but that we treat the search for the truth as being the driving force of our lives. Discrimination and dispassion develop in parallel.

3. Six-fold discipline

This means control in all its aspects, from disciplining the mind not to indulge in fantasies to discipline of the senses to avoid temptation or distraction. Success here means that the mind avoids agitation. Only a still mind can see clearly and exercise discrimination. It also relates to disciplining the body and exercising discretion in what one says to others. It is not possible to turn one's mind to considerations of a spiritual nature if one's body is in pain. This is where the practice of Hatha yoga becomes relevant. Physical Yoga does not have anything to do with enlightenment in itself but it does help to ensure that the body and its mundane physical concerns do not obstruct the spiritual search.

It is also about moderation in all that we do. Excesses of eating or drinking, too much exercise or inordinate laziness should be avoided; we should aim for a balanced lifestyle in work rest and play. Similarly, we should avoid wasting time and energy in such activities as argument or gossip, speculation about the future or reminiscence over the past.

As regards the senses, it is not always possible to prevent impressions arising in the mind as a result of natural processing by one of the senses. So again discrimination and dispassion are needed.

As regards the mind, we also require discrimination to help us avoid those situations which might prove stressful. Since this is not always possible, the mind must be trained to be able to cope with such conditions. We need to have the clarity and composure necessary to enable us to be able to focus on what really matters, filtering out extraneous irrelevancies. And we need to be able to recognize which are those activities which will lead us towards our ultimate goal (i.e. to gain self-knowledge) and which will take us away. We need to have the patience to be able to cope with those inevitable circumstances which are not conducive, simply doing whatever is necessary to clear them and make way for those activities which are helpful. All of this necessitates both restraint and concentration. It could be regarded as conserving our energy (so that it is available for pursuing what really matters and is not frittered away on the trivial) and then directing it in a controlled and efficient manner.

In conjunction with all of this, we must be patient, when

obstacles arise and have the strength to cope with these. This is one of the main reasons why religions advocate such things as fasting and pilgrimage, so as to build up our resistance to hardship and prevent our resolve from being weakened.

If we read the scriptures or, if possible, listen to a qualified teacher read them to us and then carefully explain their meaning, we will need two particular traits, namely trust and concentration.

Trust in the teacher and respect for the scriptures were mentioned in Chapter 4. You are never asked to accept anything that either goes against reason or against your own experience and senses. As will be seen, the process of learning goes through three stages and, in the end you will directly appreciate the truth for yourself. But this takes time, dependent upon the readiness of the student.

Concentration is the ability to direct your attention and avoid distractions. In our modern age, this seems to be a skill that is becoming less common. Certainly, documentary programs on TV seem to expect, as a matter of course, that viewers will not be able to assimilate anything unless the content is presented in bite-sized quanta, supported by computerized graphics and music. One tweet message and the mind needs to switch to something else.

4. Desire for Liberation

This is the driving force behind all of the above. It is this that is colloquially spoken of as putting one's head in the tiger's mouth (once in, it doesn't come out again). It has to be the only important thing in one's life, with everything else being inconsequential or, at best, peripheral. It often comes about in those people who, for most of their lives, have sought happiness and meaning in all of the traditional (and maybe even illegal) pursuits and realized the futility of ever finding them. Alternatively, a key life-changing experience, perhaps involving one's own near-death or some other catastrophe, may bring about a new outlook on life. It entails the belief that one is limited and doomed and the desperate wish to escape.

Three Stages of Learning

There are three phases to jnana yoga, the process of acquiring Self-knowledge. These are called shravana, manana and nididhyasana.

1. Hearing the truth from a qualified teacher or (very much second best) reading about it in such works as the Upanishads. This is called shravana, resulting in a basic understanding of the subject matter.

2. Reflecting upon what has been heard. This is the stage of manana, the purpose being to remove any doubts, and resolve any conflicting explanations we may harbor about the teaching.

3. Meditating upon the essence of what has now been fully understood until there is total conviction. This is called nididhyasana. It has the effect of eroding all of the bad habits we have acquired in respect of our dealings with the world, seeing separation, having desires for objects etc.

It is possible, of course, that on hearing the words 'You are That (non-dual Brahman)' for the first time, a seeker will instantly realize the truth of the statement, in the same way that you understand immediately that the film star is the spotty oik you knew at school – but it is extremely unlikely. For most people, the process of listening, reflecting, meditating on, has to be repeated many times. Even the Upanishad that uses this phrase repeats it nine times, to hammer home the message.

Jivanmukti

Theoretically, it is possible to realize the truth simply by hearing it but it is usually necessary to seek clarification by asking questions - hence the desirability of a teacher, since a book may not answer your specific questions. Although you may become enlightened after shravana and manana, you are unlikely to gain the full benefits - the so-called 'fruit of knowledge' or jnana phalam. Whether you do or not depends upon the extent to which you completed the preparatory stages described above. If your mind was totally prepared, then enlightenment gives rise to total peace and acceptance of whatever one's remaining life may bring. Otherwise, one's habitual tendencies, feelings of dissatisfaction and so on may continue. In order to overcome these, further nididhyasana will be necessary. This may take the form of continuing to read the scriptures, attend classes, possibly teach others if one has the skills etc. Ultimately, the benefits will be gained and such a person is then called a jivanmukti. Such a one may be recognized not just because of inner peace and knowledge but also outward love and compassion for all. Irrespective of whether this stage is reached, an enlightened person is not reborn.

9

Why is traditional Advaita so powerful?

Advaita uses a number of what are called 'prakriyas' as part of the traditional teaching. These are particular ways of explaining key aspects which have been proven to work and have been passed down from teacher to disciple over the centuries.

The most famous 'great saying' in the Upanishads is an effective equation. The Sanskrit is 'tat tvam asi' and it means 'You are That'. What this saying is that who you essentially are is identical to Brahman, the non-dual reality or, if you want to put it more dramatically - 'You are God'. At first sight, you are most unlikely to be convinced by this! The meaning has to be 'unfolded' by a skilled teacher using the prakriyas from the Upanishads.

An arithmetical example

A simple example from arithmetic will illustrate the idea of a prakriya. Suppose that a child is able to recognize and use numbers as a means for counting but has not yet been introduced to arithmetic. The teacher presents the child with the following equation, explaining that the two sides of the equal sign are identical:

$$5 + 7 = 3 \times 4$$

The child sees the numbers and signs and argues as follows: The left-hand side contains the numbers 5 and 7 and a character '+', whose meaning he does not yet appreciate. The right-hand side contains two totally different numbers, 3 and 4, together with an entirely different character 'x', which he may well recognize as a letter. Clearly, he reasons, the two sides of the '=' sign are entirely different. How can you possibly claim that they are identical?

The teacher then asks the child to put these considerations entirely to one side for a moment. He explains the meaning of the '+' sign and shows how the mathematical procedure of addition works, eventually showing that, if you treat the left-hand side as an addition sum, you can calculate the 'answer' to be '12'.

Later, as a separate exercise, he asks the child to look at the right-hand side and he explains the principle of multiplication. Eventually, the child can work out that the right-hand side evaluates to the answer '12'.

Now there is no further need for any explanation. The identity of the two sides of the equation is self-evident.

So now we can return to the claim that 'You are That (non-dual reality)'. You are now in the same position as the child presented with the arithmetical equation above. You know that you are a separate, suffering individual ('little me'), here but for a short time and destined to return to dust all too soon. Life is known to be 'solitary, poor, nasty, brutish and short' as Thomas Hobbes put it. The 'totality' is infinite, eternal, all-knowing, all-powerful etc. What could be more different and how can we even countenance such an outrageous claim?

So, in just the same way as the child, we are asked to put aside such beliefs, since holding on to them will only cause problems. If we are constantly throwing up our arms and objecting that 5 does not equal 3 and 7 does not equal 4, it will not help us to assimilate what the teacher is saying.

The teacher now takes the left-hand side and leads us through reasoning and scriptural unfoldment until we eventually come to the realization that my essential nature is Consciousness. He then takes the right-hand side and, quite independently leads us to the understanding that the nature of reality itself is Consciousness alone. Then, the identity of the two sides becomes self-evident and no further explanation is required.

The Sheath Model

What I will do for the remainder of this chapter is look at a particular model presented in one of the Upanishads (Taittiriya). This is not because it is one of my favorite metaphors but because it illustrates several of these prakriyas, techniques or formulae.

Simplistically, this is the idea that there are various levels of identification of 'Who I really am' with aspects of the body-mind and that these have to be recognized and dropped so that I can realize my true nature. At the outset, I should warn you that there is often a serious misunderstanding on the part of the seeker who, taking the metaphor in a more literal sense, mistakenly believes that the self is literally 'covered over' by these 'layers' and somehow has to be 'uncovered', like some Russian doll. This is NOT the case.

The first of these 'sheaths' – the 'grossest' and the one with which we first tend to identify - is the body. This is referred to as the sheath made of food. The body is born, grows old, dies and decays back into the food from which it originally came (well, food for worms anyway) but this has nothing to do with the real Self, which is much closer than hand or skin.

The second layer is called the 'vital sheath' or sheath made of breath . Hindu mythology refers to the 'air' as breathing life into the body. We might call it the vital force by means of which the body is animated and actions are performed. Although this force derives from the Self, as indeed everything does, it is not the Self. (Remember we are talking at the level of vyavahara!) We each of us tend to believe that we are somehow immortal. Although we acknowledge that the body must eventually die we feel that there is this animating force which will survive that death. This is the identification with the vital sheath.

The next layer is the mental sheath consisting of the thinking mind and the organs of perception. The function of this part of the mental makeup is to mediate between the body and the 'outside world', as opposed to the intellect. The intellect is the higher faculty of mind, responsible for discrimination, recognizing truth or falsehood, real or unreal, without recourse to mundane things like thought and memory. In silence, it knows without needing to think.

The final sheath is called the 'Bliss' sheath. Some readers who meditate may have been fortunate enough to experience moments of the most profound peace and silence, when the mind is completely absent and a feeling of deep contentment can be felt. It might be thought that this is the state of realization for which we are aiming, if only it could be maintained. Instead it only usually lasts a few minutes for most of us, although Indian ascetics are reputed to enter such states for very much longer periods. But this is just another sheath, albeit perhaps a desirable and blissful one. We are still observing it and therefore cannot be it.

What we truly are, then, is the 'Real Self' or simply 'Self' with a capital 'S'. But, through identification with these various layers or sheaths, this Self is obscured. It is like water contained in a colored glass bottle. The water itself seems to take on the color of the glass, though it is itself colorless.

Discrimination between the Seer and the Seen

We looked at the intellectual exercise of discriminating what we might initially think we are from who we really are in an earlier chapter. One of the Upanishads famously has a section in which the phrase 'neti, neti' (not this, not this) is used for this purpose. This sort of differentiation is called Discrimination between the Self and not-Self. Practically speaking, if we recognize that I, the subject, cannot be this body, mind etc because I am seeing it as an object, then this is an example of Discrimination between the Seer and the Seen.

The exercise has two aspects. Firstly, one rejects the perceived objects or body-mind etc as 'not me'. Secondly, one recognizes that there is something that remains unchanging and present throughout all of these experiences, namely 'I' the witness. The body, for example, grows old and dies – but 'I' remain the same.

Arundhati logic

Another method which is being used here is one which directs our attention to increasingly more subtle levels so that, although we may not appreciate what is meant by the Atman initially, we do by the end.

It is called 'Arundhati logic' after the Indian name given to a star, Alcor, in the constellation of Ursa Major (Great Bear, Plough or Big Dipper). It is one of the clearest examples of the Advaitic method of teaching.

In marriage ceremonies in India, the star is pointed out to the bride as an example to be followed, since the star is "devoted" to its companion star, Mizar or Vasishtha (Arundhati was the wife of Vasishtha). Because the star is scarcely visible, it is necessary to lead the eye to it gradually. Thus one might first locate the constellation by reference to the moon. Then the attention can be directed to the bright star that is at the tail of the Great Bear. Finally, there is a companion star which is only 11 minutes distant and fourth magnitude that can only be seen by people with exceptional eyesight. This is Arundhati.

In the same way, in this Sheath Model, the TaittirIya Upanishad first points to the body as being the Atman but then indicates that the vital energy is more subtle and the body is, after all, only food. In this way, the disciple is guided through successive levels until he is able to recognize his previously mistaken identifications and understand his essential nature.

It is also an example of the principal method of Advaita – adhyaropa-apavada introduced in the chapter on 'World'. First we are told that we are the body. This is then shown to be an erroneous superimposition due to ignorance and that explanation is taken back. Then it is said we are the life-force, prana. Then that is shown to be wrong and rejected. And so on until we finally appreciate that we must be the Atman.

Shankara comments on the model: "The individual soul, though intrinsically none other than Brahman, still identifies itself with, and becomes attached to, the sheaths made of food etc, which are external, limited, and composed of the subtle elements." And he refers to the Tenth Man story described earlier. In the same way, "the individual soul, under a spell of ignorance characterized by the non-perception of one's own true nature as Brahman, accepts the external non-Selves, such as the body composed of food, as the Self, and as a consequence, begins to think, 'I am none other than those non-Selves composed of food etc.'"

In practice, of course, we do not consciously identify with the sheath itself but with one or more attributes of them. Thus, for example, we claim that 'I am stupid', effectively identifying with the mind or intellect. The Self is never really associated with these attributes or the sheaths themselves because only the Self is real – the rest are mithya. Failure to understand this leads some teachers to claim that we need to 'get rid of the mind' or 'destroy the ego' in order to achieve realization. This is like saying that we have to kill the snake in order to discover the rope.

Method of Co-presence and Co-absence

Finally, this model is also an example of the Method of Co-presence and Co-absence (anvaya – vyatireka). The physical body is absent in the dream state although 'I' am present in both states. Therefore, I am not the body. The subtle body is similarly absent in deep sleep, though 'I' remain. Therefore, I cannot be the vital, mental or intellectual sheath either. Finally, ignorance (which equates to the bliss sheath) disappears in the state of samadhi (a rarefied, meditative state, claimed to be the ultimate aim in Yoga philosophy) so that I cannot be this sheath either.

In fact, I am the Atman, present in all three states, witnessing the so-called sheaths. They are only coverings to the extent that, through ignorance, I take myself to be other than Atman. I say that 'I am fat', 'I am old' etc because I take myself to be the physical body. Therefore, effectively, the body acts as a 'covering' over my true nature. But these are attributes of the body, not my Self. The Atman does not itself have any of these attributes; and likewise for the other sheaths.

The key thing to realize, warns Swami Dayananda (probably the greatest living teacher of Advaita at the time of writing), is that there is not some 'inner Self' to be experienced beyond or inside of all these sheaths. We are that Atman all the time, no matter what mistaken view the mind might be taking. Nothing is ever really 'hidden'.

10

What different approaches are there?

Categories of Teaching

The teaching of Advaita falls into four main categories (these were introduced in Chapter 8):

1. **Traditional**, or so-called sampradaya teaching. The word 'sampradaya' means that the methods and understanding have been handed down from teacher to disciple for literally thousands of years. Since it was Shankara who effectively formulated the guidelines based upon all of the extant material at the time, modern sampradaya teachers should be able to trace their lineage back to him. Disciples usually stay at an ashram for several years (at least) and attend talks, meditate, etc. every day. It is this teaching which forms the principal subject matter of this book.

2. **Neo-Vedanta.** This is a later development of traditional teaching and, nowadays, probably has more teachers. It stems from Vivekananda, who following his own guidance from the 19th Century mystic Ramakrishna, strove to bring Vedanta to the West, a mission in which he had some considerable success. The teaching which he promoted incorporated some aspects from Yoga. This is itself a distinct philosophy, so inevitably some of the principles of Advaita Vedanta have been changed. In particular, an emphasis is placed on samadhi, even though Advaita points out that this is simply another experience that cannot bring about Self-knowledge. This insistence may also be a consequence of the fact that Ramakrishna himself

regularly experienced samadhi throughout his life.

3. **Western Satsang**. In its traditional use, the word literally means 'association with the wise or good' and refers to a group of true seekers led by a qualified teacher. It denotes a meeting in which some teaching is given, followed by question and answer. (In traditional teaching, it refers only to the question and answer session itself.) In the West, it is now common for a 'teacher' to travel around the world holding short meetings in which, very often, there is no real teaching at all, simply the answering of random questions. I have called this Western style of pseudo-teaching 'satsang' teaching in my earlier books.

4. **Neo-advaita**. This is a relatively modern development (perhaps as recent as the 1980s) and refers to the style of teaching that purports to express only the final, absolute truth of advaita. It does not admit of any 'levels' of reality and does not recognize the existence of a seeker, teacher, ignorance, spiritual path etc. Whereas satsang teachers in general differ quite widely as regards their particular ways of talking about and teaching advaita, neo-advaitin teachers do not. The statements of one are essentially inter-changeable with those of another, with only personal style and coined phrases differing.

And, lest there still be any doubt about the meaning of the word 'enlightenment', here is a definition:

Enlightenment

It is self-ignorance that prevents recognition of the truth about our nature and that of reality. Enlightenment takes place in the mind of a person when self-ignorance has been eradicated. It is true (in absolute reality) that we are already 'free' - there is only ever the non-dual reality so how could it be otherwise? It is not true that we are already enlightened (in empirical reality), as the seeker well knows. Enlightenment is the event in time when the mind realizes that we are already free.

Rather than 'reinventing the wheel', I would like to borrow the conclusions from my book Enlightenment: the Path through the Jungle to summarize the key points about teaching and enlightenment:

Over the past 30 – 40 years, there has been an accelerating trend in the West towards the use of the satsang as the sole method for teaching Advaita. This probably stems from the popularity of the transcriptions of talks by Ramana Maharshi and Nisargadatta Maharaj but gained momentum when many new teachers claimed the blessing of Sri Poonja. (Note that these are all well known teachers from the 20th Century. The first two are justifiably renowned as transcriptions of their talks carry considerable wisdom.) Traditionally, a sampradaya teacher would only authorize disciples as teachers in their own right when he had been able to confirm their enlightened status and verify their complete under-standing of the teaching methods of the scriptures. Today, scarcely any satsang teacher in the West can claim this authority. (Note that only Nisargadatta belonged to a sampradaya, but his style of teaching was very much satsang.)

In neo-Advaita, the traditional teaching has been impoverished to the point of extinction with nothing remaining of its wealth of methods and its ability to cater for all levels and types of seeker. Instead, all that remains are abstruse statements about the nature of absolute reality, which are only really meaningful to the most advanced student. Since most of the seekers attending these meetings are not advanced, their confusion and suffering is exacer-bated rather than relieved.

Increasingly, it seems that other satsang teachers are also moving in this direction. This may well be the natural consequence of the format of the satsang being ill-suited to genuine teaching. Since seekers attend only occasional meetings, often with different teachers and usually with different students, there is no continuity and the message needs to be conveyed in a short time. Western society also wants (and expects) instant results.

The fundamental problem is the self-ignorance in the mind of the seeker as a result of adhyasa. Appropriate knowledge is needed and this has to be acceptable to the mind, which must be able to exercise reason and discrimination, not be confounded by past opinions and beliefs and so on. All of this takes place naturally as part of the traditional teaching process under the guidance of a skilled teacher. Clearly, at the level of the world, there are seekers who do things. Ideally, they should prepare the mind through appropriate practices and follow a formal, proven, logical path to gain self-knowledge, with the help of a competent guide. Only on successful completion will they fully realize that they always have been Brahman. All of this is in direct contradiction to the teaching of neo-advaita.

Where there is darkness, light is needed. Traditional teaching provides that light in the form of gradual, structured, tailored and reasoned explanation that can be verified in our own experience and must lead ultimately to realization of the truth. Neo-advaita attempts to bypass all of this and present the final conclusion without any arguments. Lacking the logic, it also proves ineffectual. The less absolutist satsang teaching may attempt to utilize some of the methodology of traditional teaching but, lacking the structure, context and continuity, it too is doomed to failure in the majority of cases.

Most satsang teachers also appear to stress the negative aspects – neti, neti; not the body, mind, ego etc. - and their end-point is that what is left is who you really are. The fact is, though, that the nature of this 'what is left' is not usually explained. The result is that seekers are given a relatively nihilistic view of reality. In the case of neo-advaita, this combines with the view that, since there is no one to do anything and the world is an illusion anyway, then whatever we might do makes no difference. Thus, for some people, an amoral outlook might be considered a logical result of hearing such teachings.

This is entirely opposite to the traditional approach, in which pointers to who we are (Brahman) are given. The famous statement from the Upanishads - 'tat tvam asi' (You are That) - dismantles our erroneous concepts about 'you' but at the same time emphasizes that we are 'That' so there is never any question of a void or emptiness. On the contrary, who we are is full and complete and limitless.

Many of these modern teachers attempt to argue that their teaching is appropriate to the time, that the scriptures are no longer relevant and that our educated and sophisticated minds can accept the final truths now without the traditional circumlocutions and indirection. In fact, our present-day self-ignorance is the same as it has always been. We still identify with body, mind and roles and still believe that there is a real world of separate objects and other people. It is these fundamental issues that are addressed by traditional methods – what we are not and what we are. The sampradayas have proven techniques for resolving these issues. Simply stating the conclusions, as neo-advaitin teachers do, will never be effective since those conclusions are quite contradictory to our present understanding of our everyday experience.

Because most modern teachers lack the formal, traditional background of authenticity; because of the casual format of satsang and the attenuated teaching content, it is becoming increasingly easy for anyone to set themselves up as a teacher without actually having any credentials – and there is no 'college of licensed advaitin teachers' which we can check.

Seekers and teachers alike need to reconcile themselves to the fact that there can be no short-term measures. We have generations of wrong thinking to rectify so that we may learn to look at ourselves and the world in a completely different way that contradicts our present beliefs. Instinct, habit and deeply-held opinion can never be overturned by a brief question and answer session on no particular *topic by individuals, each with their own agenda. It requires a prolonged, coordinated inquiry, using proven techniques, with the help of teachers skilled in using those techniques. Genuine seekers of the truth must find a teaching environment that satisfies these requirements.*

Conclusion

The final message you should take away from this book was quoted in a different form at the beginning; it is very simple:

Reality is non-dual.
The world is mithya.
I am that non-dual reality.

What should you read to find out more?

If you go into your local bookstore, it is most likely that you will find no books at all on this subject (although, hopefully, this book might be the one exception, since it is one of a series of 'Made Easy' books). You may be surprised, therefore, to hear that there is a vast body of literature available if you actively search for it. Most of the books originate from India, and are only available there. And probably most of them have never been translated into English. Many are still in their original Sanskrit.

Accordingly, if you look on the Internet and pick out a few relevant books at random, it is very likely that you will be disappointed. You may choose material that is quite unhelpful and maybe even totally unreadable. Unfortunately, there are also many writers and teachers out there who have no real understanding of what they are talking about - these are the most dangerous of all, since it will be a cease of 'the blind leading the blind'.

The books available may be categorized as follows:

1. Authoritative Traditional

There are three main sources for these:

- Upanishads - these usually occur towards the end of the vast body of Hindu scriptures called the Vedas.
- the Bhagavad Gita - this forms a part of the Hindu epic story called the Mahabharata and effectively consists of a question and answer dialog on key aspects of the philosophy.
- The Brahma Sutras, together with Shankara's commentary. In this, questions and doubts arising from the first source are raised and resolved and contradictory interpretations are refuted.

2. Classical explanatory texts by Shankara, his direct disciples and others

There are many of these and some of those attributed to Shankara are disputed. Most of them are much more approachable than the works in the first category and some have become justifiably popular, such as the Vivekachudamani (Crest Jewel of Discrimination).

3. Works by modern sages, such as Ramana Maharshi and Nisargadatta Maharaj

These are often not written by the sage in question but consist of transcriptions by disciples of what was said by the sage, usually in answer to specific questions. Here we enter one of the principal problems of many books about Advaita. If the work is not written by someone who has directly realized the truth for themselves; if it is not written as a complete explanation from first principles; if instead, it is addressing specific questions from a particular person who has a particular problem - then it is likely that you will not understand what is said in the way that it was intended. This is not to say that such books are without value - some, indeed, are excellent - but these potential shortcomings must always be borne in mind.

4. Books by modern teachers.

It seems that most modern western teachers, of whichever category, are attempting to circumvent the introductory explanations and mental preparation and present the 'bottom line' conclusions of Advaita. This is not possible and only leads to frustration. Fortunately, there are still a few traditional teachers who follow the proven methods of the past and whose books and recorded talks may be relied upon. Most of these are associated with the organizations set up by Swamis Chinmayananda and Dayananda or with the Neo-

Vedanta organizations of Ramakrishna, Vivekananda and Sarada Devi.

5. Modern explanatory texts.

These are attempts to expound the overall philosophy, rather like this book but in much more depth. Some are intentionally academic in nature while others are aimed at the serious seeker.

My website - www.advaita.org.uk - has a section which aims to provide detailed reviews for all currently published books on Advaita, indicating such aspects as target audience, Sanskrit content, readability and do on. But I provide below a very brief set of recommendations in each of the above categories.

1a) For a clear presentation and explanation of four of the principal Upanishads, suitable for beginners, I recommend **Choice Upanishads**, written and published by A. Parthasarathy, ISBN 8187111607. (The 'principal' Upanishads are the 12 for which Shankara provided a commentary. There are around 108 in total, many more having been lost.)

For a readable and guaranteed authoritative (i.e. according to sampradaya teaching) explanation of one of the key upanishads, taken from his talks on this: **Mundaka Upanishad**, by Swami Dayananda, in two volumes published by Arsha Vidya Centre, ISBN 81-903636-3-8 and 81-903636-5-4.

1b) There are literally hundreds of translations and commentaries on the Bhagavad Gita. I presently have 22 of these in the Advaita Vision library but have not actually read them all! I would not recommend a 'straight' translation for the beginner, especially those which present the original Sanskrit together with word by word analysis. Instead, there are a number of books which address the essence of the work, rather than the actual verses. Swami Dayananda (any of whose books can be recommended, although some contain too much Sanskrit for the beginner) has written the excellent introduction **The Teaching of the Bhagavad Gita**, Vision Books, ISBN 817094032X. In it, he chooses specific verses in order to highlight the key issues.

A supremely readable commentary for the modern reader, which does include each verse, is **The Living Gita** by Sri Swami Satchidananda, Integral Yoga Publications, ISBN 0932040276. Strictly speaking, this is Yoga rather than Advaita but that really does not matter too much – it is full of clearly expressed wisdom.

1c) I do not recommend that any beginning student of Advaita attempt to read any presentation of the Brahma Sutras. These are for much later study!

2. The classical introductory texts attributed to Shankara are Tattva Bodha, Atma Bodha and Vivekachudamani.

The **Tattva bodha** explains all of the terminology that will be encountered as you proceed with your studies and I have to confess shamefacedly that I have not read this myself! The version that you will be able to purchase is that translated by Swami Tejomayananda, published by Central Chinmaya Mission Trust, ISBN 9788175971851.

Shankara's Crest Jewel of Discrimination, translated by Swami Prabhavananda and Christopher Isherwood, Vedanta Press, ISBN 0874810388, presents the essence of the Vivekachudamani in clear English without reference to individual verses or

Sanskrit. It is extremely readable and covers many of the main concepts and teachings.

3. The problem with modern sages (with a few exceptions) is that their teaching is sometimes too individualistic or even eccentric. This may be because they are answering a particular seeker's question, as noted above, but may also be because they themselves were not part of a traditional guru-disciple lineage. Accordingly, there is a danger that the seeker may be misled by what is said and, strictly speaking, the beginner ought not to dip into books by these teachers.

Providing this danger is noted, however, two justifiably acclaimed modern books may be mentioned.

Be As You Are: The Teachings of Sri Ramana Maharshi, edited by David Godman, Penguin, ISBN 0140190627. Short, but full of the wonderfully clear teachings of probably the most important teacher of the past millennium. This can be recommended whole heartedly as one of the very best books on Advaita. David Godman researched many sources and combined the material so as to provide fuller answers to the various questions, which are sorted into topics.

I am That – Discourses by Nisargadatta Maharaj, translated by Maurice Frydman, Acorn Press, ISBN 0893860220. This is probably the best known book by any modern day Sage and justly so. It consists of short dialogues that he had with visitors, who traveled from around the world to listen to his blunt and forceful answers to questions on a variety of topics of concern to those still trapped in the illusory world. There are many wonderful, direct and unambiguous statements from this illiterate seller of cigars in the back streets of Mumbai.

4. There are quite a number of so-called 'satsang' teachers in the West today, who travel around the world holding short meetings of a couple of hours at which they answer questions from seekers. Some also hold longer sessions of one or two days or even week-long 'residential' courses. Because of the nature of these meetings, such teachers do not have true disciples who absorb the teachings over many years of regular classes. Accordingly the guru-seeker relationship is never established and any teaching is entirely ad hoc, being dependent upon the nature of the questions that happen to arise during the meeting.

It is clear from their books that some of these teachers have deep understanding of the material but it is equally clear that many do not and, in any case, occasional satsang attendance is totally inadequate for the vast majority of seekers.

Two books in particular, however, provide excellent general reading on the subject of Advaita and can be highly recommended.

A Natural Awakening by Philip Mistlberger, TigerFyre Publishing, ISBN 0973341904, looks at the perceived problems of the seeker from the standpoint of Western psychology and shows how Advaita resolves them and leads to understanding of one's true nature. This book was self-published, so you may have difficulty obtaining a copy.

How to Attain Enlightenment: The Vision of Nonduality by James Swartz, Sentient Publications, ISBN 978-1591810940. James was a close associate of Swami Chinmayananda and has been teaching traditionally-based Advaita to Western students for several decades. He is passionate about it and speaks and writes lucidly on the subject. Much wisdom has been packed into this book and it can be highly recommended.

5. I am obliged to cast modesty aside here and claim that the best book in this category is the second edition of my own **The Book of One: The Ancient Wisdom of Advaita**, O Books, ISBN 978-1846943478. I originally wrote this in 2002 in order to clarify in my own mind exactly what Advaita was saying. And I deliberately wrote it in an entertaining manner in the hope that it might appeal to others as well. But I still had some misunderstandings as a result of the manner in which I first learned about the subject, and it was not until I began to read much more widely and discuss topics with others more knowledgeable than myself that I slowly cleared up these misunderstandings. Accordingly, I was able to correct these and add a lot more explanatory material, metaphors and quotations in this new edition in 2010. Accordingly, I know of no better book to read if you wish to find out more about what has been discussed in this book.

Glossary

adhyasa – used to refer to the 'mistake' that we make when we 'superimpose' a false appearance upon the reality or mix up the real and the unreal. The classical example is when we see a snake instead of a rope, which is used as a metaphor for seeing the world of objects instead of the reality of the Self. This concept is fundamental to Advaita and Shankara devotes a separate section to it at the beginning of his commentary on the Brahmasutra.

advaita – not (*a*) duality (*dvaita*); non-dual teaching methodology based on Vedanta.

agamin – That type of *sanskara* or *karma* which is generated in reaction to current situations and which will not bear fruit until sometime in the future. It literally means 'impending,' 'approaching' or 'coming.' See *prarabdha, sanchita, sanskara, karma*.

ahankara – the making, *kara*, of the utterance 'I,' *aham* – the 'I' thought and everything appended to it.

ajati – *a* – no or not; *jati* – birth or production; the principle that the world and everything in it, including these mind-body appearances were never created or 'brought into existence'. The theory that there has never been any creation is called either *ajata vada* or *ajati vada*.

asatkarya vada – the doctrine which denies that the effect pre-exists in the cause (usually in reference to the creation).

atman – the Self. Usually used to refer to one's true (individual) nature or consciousness but Advaita tells us that there is no such thing as an 'individual' and that this *Atman* is the same as the universal Consciousness, *brahman*. see also *jiva*.

avarana – the veiling power of *maya*, which brings about the ignorance that prevents us from seeing the truth. See *maya, vikshepa*.

avidya – ignorance (in a spiritual sense) i.e. that which prevents us from realizing the Self. See also *maya*.

Bhagavad Gita – the scriptural text forming part of the Hindu epic, the Mahabarata. It is a dialogue between Krishna, the charioteer/God, representing the Self and the warrior Arjuna, representing you and me, on the battlefield of Kurukshetra prior to the commencement of battle.

bhakti yoga – devotion or worship as a preparatory dicipline to enlightenment. See also *karma* and *jnana*.

Brahman – the universal Self, Absolute or God. There is only *brahman*. It derives from the Sanskrit root *bRRih*, meaning to grow great or strong and could be thought of as the adjective 'big' made into a noun, implying that which is greater than anything. See also *atman, jiva*.

Brahmasutra – a book (in sutra form, which is terse verse!) by Vyasa. Effectively, it attempts to summarize the Upanishads. It has been extensively commented on by the three main branches of Vedanta, *dvaita, advaita* and *vishishtadvaita*, and the proponents of each claim that it substantiates their beliefs. Shankara has commented on it and provided extensive arguments against any interpretation other than that of Advaita..

dharma – customary practice, conduct, duty, justice and morality. See *sanskara, karma*.

dvaita – duality, philosophy of dualism; belief that God, the universe and the *atman* are separate entities. Madhva is the scholar most often associated with this philosophy.

Gaudapada – The author of the commentary on the Mandukya Upanishad. He is said to have been the teacher of Shankara's teacher.

guru – literally 'heavy'; used to refer to one's elders or a person of reverence but more commonly in the West to indicate one's spiritual teacher. Traditionally, such a person must be both enlightened and knowledgeable in the scriptures.

Ishvara – the Lord; creator of the phenomenal universe.

jiva – the identification of the *atman* with a body and mind; sometimes spoken of as 'the embodied *atman*.' See *atman*.

jIvanmukta – an enlightened person who has also acquired the fruits of Self-knowledge. (*mukta* is the adjective – liberated; *mukti* is the noun – liberation)

jnana yoga – *yoga* based on the acquisition of true knowledge (*j~nAna* means 'knowledge') i.e. knowledge of the Self as opposed to mere information about the world of appearances. See also *bhakti, karma, yoga*.

karma – literally 'action' but generally used to refer to the 'law' whereby actions carried out now will have their lawful effects in the future (and this may be in future lives). Note that *karma yoga* is something different – see below. See also *sanskara*.

karma yoga – A devotional attitude to action whereby the grip of attachments and aversions is loosened and one's mind is thus prepared for the acquisition of self-knowledge. See *bhakti, karma, jnana, yoga*.

lila – literally 'play,' 'amusement' or 'pastime'; the idea that the apparent creation is a diversion for a creator – a means for Him to enjoy Himself. He plays all the parts in such a way that they are ignorant of their real nature and believe themselves separate.

manana– reflecting upon what has been heard (*shravana*). This is the second stage of the classical spiritual path, to remove any doubts about the knowledge that has been received via *shravana*. See also *shravana, nididhyasana*.

maya– literally 'magic' or 'witchcraft'. The 'force' used to explain how it is that we come to be deceived into believing that there is a creation with separate objects and living creatures etc. See also *avarana* and *vikshepa*.

mithya – dependent reality; literally 'incorrectly' or 'improperly,' used in the sense of 'false, untrue.' It is, however, more frequently used in the sense of 'depending upon something else for its existence.' It is ascribed to objects etc., meaning that these are not altogether unreal but not strictly real either i.e. they are our imposition of name and form upon the undifferentiated Self. See *adhyasa*.

moksha – liberation from the sense of limitation centered on 'I'; enlightenment, Self-realization.

neti – Literally, "No!", usually translated as 'not this'. Used by the intellect whenever it is thought that the Self might be some 'thing' observed e.g. body, mind etc. The Self cannot be anything that is seen, thought or known.

nididhyasana – meditating upon myself as the essence of all, returning the mind from where it has habitually strayed to what has now been understood, until there is total conviction of the non-difference between my self and the self of all. The third stage of the classical spiritual path. See also *shravana* and *manana*.

paramartha (noun), *paramarthika* (adj.) – the highest truth or reality; the noumenal as opposed to the phenomenal world of appearances. See *pratibhasa* and *vyavahara*.

prarabdha – This literally means 'begun' or 'undertaken.' It is the fruit of all of our past action that is now having its effect. This is one of the three types of *sanskara or karmas*. See *agamin*, *sanchita, sanskara*.

pratibhAsa (noun), *prAtibhAsika* (adj.) – appearing or occurring to the mind, existing only in appearance, an illusion or dream. See *paramartha, vyavahara*.

samadhi – the state of total peace and stillness achieved during deep meditation.

sankhya – one of the three main divisions of Hindu philosophy.

sampradaya – the tradition or established doctrine of teaching from *guru* to disciple through the ages.

samsara – the continual cycle of death and rebirth, transmigration etc. to which we are subject in the phenomenal world until we become enlightened and escape.

sanchita – one of the three types of *sanskara* or *karmas*, literally meaning 'collected' or 'piled up.' That *sanskara*, which has been accumulated from past action but has still not manifest. See *agamin, prarabdha, sanskara.*

sanskara – Whenever an action is performed, *sanskara* or *karmas* result. These invisible fruits of action accumulate and determine the situations with which we will be presented in the future and will influence the scope of future actions. There are three 'types' – *agamin, sanchita* and *prarabdha.* See *agamin, karma, prarabdha, sanchita.*

satkarya vada – the doctrine of the effect actually pre-existing in the cause (usually in reference to the creation) This is the belief of the *sankhya* system of philosophy.

satsanga – association with the good; keeping 'good company'; most commonly used now to refer to a group of people gathered together to discuss (Advaita) philosophy.

Shankara – 8th Century Indian philosopher responsible for firmly establishing the principles of Advaita. Though he died at an early age (32?), he commented on a number of major Upanishads, the Bhagavad Gita and the Brahmasutras, as well as being attributed as the author of a number of famous works, such as Atmabodha, Bhaja Govindam and Vivekachudamani.

shravana – hearing the truth from a sage or reading about it in such works as the Upanishads; first of the three key stages in the classical spiritual path. See also *manana, nididhyasana.*

upanishad – one of the (108+) books forming part (usually the end) of one of the four Vedas. The parts of the word mean: to sit (*shad*) near a master (*upa*) at his feet (*ni*), so that the idea is that we sit at the feet of a master to listen to his words. See Vedanta.

upasana – worship, homage, waiting upon; literally the act of sitting or being near to; sometimes used in the sense of 'meditation.'

vada – speech, proposition, discourse, argument, discussion, explanation or exposition (of scriptures etc.)

veda – knowledge, but the word is normally only used to refer to one of the four Vedas (see Vedanta) and *vidya* is used for knowledge per se. See *vidya*.

Vedanta – literally 'end' or 'culmination' (*anta*) of the Vedas (*veda*), referring to the four Vedas, the Hindu equivalents of the Christian bible. Traditionally, the last part of the *veda-s* (i.e. 'end') is devoted to the Upanishads. See *upanishad*.

vidya – knowledge, science, learning, philosophy. *atma-vidya* or *brahma-vidya* is knowledge of the Self.

vikshepa – the 'projecting' power of *maya*, which produces the world of plurality like a film on a cinema screen. See *avarana*, *maya*.

vivarta vada – the theory that the world is only an apparent projection of Ishvara (i.e. an illusion).

viveka – discrimination; the ability to differentiate between the unreal and the real.

vyavahAra **(noun)**, *vyAvahArika* **(adj.)** – the 'relative,' 'practical,' or phenomenal world of appearances; the transactional world in which we live and which we usually believe to be real; as opposed to *paramartha* (reality) and *pratibhasa* (illusory). See *paramartha* and *pratibhasa*.

yoga – literally 'joining' or 'attaching' (our word 'yoke' derives from this). It is used generally to refer to any system whose aim is to 'join' our 'individual self' back to the 'universal Self.' A yoga is therefore anything that prepares the mind for the knowledge of the non-difference between individual and universal self. The Yoga system of philosophy pedantically refers to that specified by Patanjali, and this differs from Advaita in a number of respects (it is, for example, dualistic!) See *bhakti, jnana, karma*.

Index

BOOKS

O is a symbol of the world, of oneness and unity. In different cultures it also means the "eye," symbolizing knowledge and insight. We aim to publish books that are accessible, constructive and that challenge accepted opinion, both that of academia and the "moral majority."

Our books are available in all good English language bookstores worldwide. If you don't see the book on the shelves ask the bookstore to order it for you, quoting the ISBN number and title. Alternatively you can order online (all major online retail sites carry our titles) or contact the distributor in the relevant country, listed on the copyright page.

See our website **www.o-books.net** for a full list of over 500 titles, growing by 100 a year.

And tune in to myspiritradio.com for our book review radio show, hosted by June-Elleni Laine, where you can listen to the authors discussing their books.

MySpiritRadio